My Weakness:
HIS STRENGTH

BOOKS BY ROBERT C. GIRARD

Brethren, Hang Loose
Brethren, Hang Together
My Weakness: His Strength

My Weakness: HIS STRENGTH

The Personal Face of Renewal

Robert C. Girard

OF THE ZONDERVAN CORPORATION
GRAND RAPIDS, MICHIGAN 49506

MY WEAKNESS: HIS STRENGTH
The Personal Face of Renewal
Copyright © 1981 by The Zondervan Corporation
Grand Rapids, Michigan

Library of Congress Cataloging in Publication Data
Girard, Robert C
  My weakness, His strength.

  Includes bibliographical references.
  1. Christian life—1960-   2. Girard, Robert C.
I. Title.
BV4501.2.G56   248.4   80-27444
ISBN 0-310-39081-8

Designed and edited by Louise H. Rock

All rights reserved. No part of this publication may be reproduced, stored in a retrieval system, or transmitted in any form or by any means—electronic, mechanical, photocopy, recording, or otherwise—except for brief quotations in printed reviews, without prior permission of the publisher.

Printed in the United States of America

To my wife and children—
they know me,
they love me.

Contents

PROLOGUE	11
1. THE INNER FACE OF RENEWAL	19

The Stowaway, 19. God of Anger, 21. The Hiding Place, 23. Child of Anger, 23. The Child and the Ministry, 25.

2. THE DAWNING OF RIGHTEOUSNESS	29

Dawn Versus Dark, 30. Light and Healing, 33. Stepping into the Light, 34. Transparency and Modeling, 38.

3. THE WEANING	41

Weaning and Growing, 41. Mothers and Substitutes, 43. The Mother-Son Syndrome, 45. Meeting One Another's Needs, 49. The Right Sort of Independence, 50.

4. THE SECOND TIME AROUND	53
5. SEARCH FOR GIFTEDNESS (Part I)	59

Giftedness, 61. Giftedness and What I Want to Do, 64. The Desires of Your Heart, 70. Getting in Touch With the New Creation, 73.

6. SEARCH FOR GIFTEDNESS (Part II)	75

A New Dream for Ministry, 75. "What Am I Going to Be When I Grow Up?" 80. The Day My "Sabbatical" Began, 83.

7. THE PRISONER	89

The Pride That Goes Before, 90. The Terror That Roars, 90. The People-Helper, 93. An Experience of Inner Healing, 95. Truth in the Inner Chamber, 98. Symptoms of Healing, 101. To Be Continued, 103.

8. I TOOK MY DEATH WISH
   TO THE CEMETERY TODAY　　　　　　105

9. THE INCREDIBLE HOPE　　　　　　　　107
   An Aggressive Pursuit of Healing, 110. Cutting the Cord, 115. The Use of Psychological Method in the Church, 120. Conclusions from "The PIT," 122. To Be Pure in Heart, 130.

10. STRENGTH IS PERFECTED IN WEAKNESS　　135
    Power, Perfection, and Weakness, 137. Gallery of Powerlessness, 139. Power Minus Weakness Equals Trouble, 142. The Thorn, 143. At Peace With What I Am, 144. Weakness on Mission, 145. Out of the Struggle, a Song, 145.

11. THE CREATOR'S NON-VERBAL
    COMMUNICATION　　　　　　　　　　149
    A Walk in the Rain, 149. Enjoying the Simple Pleasures, 151. Celebrating the Temporary, 154. God's Body-Language, 155. The Speaking Stars, 155.

12. SPIRITUAL SICKNESS AND ITS CURE　　　159
    Death of Sovereignty, 159. Causes of Breakdown, 162. The Essence of Breakdown, 167. The Years of the Locusts, 169. Return to Sovereignty, 172.

13. BETWEEN THE RED SEA
    AND MOUNT SINAI　　　　　　　　　　179
    "The Ever-Whirling Wheels of Change," 179. Freedom Is Tough Too, 185. Arrival at Sinai, 188. Embarkation, 194.

NOTES　　　　　　　　　　　　　　　　　　195

Acknowledgments

Thanks to Larry Richards, Rod Wilke, and Christine Girard Poehls for reading the manuscript and giving helpful suggestions, most of which I have sought to incorporate in this book.

Unless otherwise noted, Scripture quotations are from *The New International Version of the Bible* (New York: New York International Bible Society, 1978).

Other translations used, as noted, are: (1) NASB, *New American Standard Bible* (Carol Stream, Ill.: Creation House, Inc., 1971), (2) *The Amplified Bible* (Grand Rapids: Zondervan Publishing House, 1965), (3) Phillips, *The New Testament in Modern English* by J. B. Phillips (New York: The MacMillan Co., First American Edition 1965, fourth printing 1968), (4) NEB, *The New English Bible* (Oxford University Press, 1970), (5) KJV, *The King James Version of the Holy Bible*.

Prologue

In 1965 Audrey and I "pioneered" a new church in Scottsdale, Arizona. It was "successful" from the start. We employed a few new ideas, but our basic mindset was quite traditional. In 1967 a jolting church business meeting unmasked us and our church for what we were: an aggregation of super-busy spiritual babies. We were involved in doing everything that a good, lively church does to be successful. But we discovered that none of it was producing true spiritual growth. Instead, like bickering children, we exchanged angry charges and counter charges. We couldn't even get along together!

A search for answers to our spiritual retardation, enhanced by the brilliantly-timed activity of God's Spirit, brought us into some fresh insights concerning the nature of the church (as the Bible describes it). The yawning chasm between what Christ intended the church to be and what it is after two millenia of human tampering seemed unbridgeable at first. But the Holy Spirit seemed to be saying, "Try. Take a few steps in the direction these biblical insights lead, and see what happens."

The "renewal story" of Our Heritage Church is told in two previous books—*Brethren, Hang Loose* (Zondervan, 1972) and *Brethren, Hang Together* (Zondervan, 1979).

We originally set out to bring structural change to the church. Our purpose was to provide a setting for the spiritual renewal of God's people, not merely to renovate the institution of the church.

> The church needs more than anything else to *know Him!* To know *the Living Son of God.* . . . To know Him

personally. To know Him in the power of His resurrection. ... Without the personal power of the Personal Jesus, there is no way to experience in a real sense the New Testament idea that in Christ "old things are passed away ... all things are become new."

To try to change the church in structure alone, hoping to bring renewal to it, without bringing its people to faith in the *Personal* Jesus, is as unthinkable as hoping that by removing the wagon tongue and adding pneumatic tires the buckboard will suddenly become self-propelled.

Making Christ personal is the key to renewal. Whatever it takes to release His resurrection life in people and through people is what it will take to bring renewal . . . whatever releases the activity of the Holy Spirit among us!

If structures hinder Him—change the structures.

If attitudes hinder Him—change the attitudes . . .

If procedures, programs, patterns, forms, approaches, methods, facilities, plans, goals, or ideals hinder Him—let them be changed!

Let the irreplaceable activity of the Spirit be released.

The great Old Testament renewal text, Second Chronicles 7:14 announces: *"If my people which are called by my name will humble themselves* (in recognition of the utter weakness and fruitlessness of the flesh), *and pray* (as an expression of dependence on the Spirit), *and seek my face* (counting everything else as loss compared to the priceless privilege of knowing the Living, Personal Jesus), *and turn from their wicked ways* (repenting of all their humanism and dependence on everything but Him—their sin)."

That will not be renewal. But renewal will result: *"Then will I hear from heaven and will forgive their sin, and will heal their land."*

That's renewal! The activity of the Holy Spirit for us, in us, among us and through us—forgiving our sin, healing our institutions, cleansing, setting us newly apart for His purpose, sanctifying, reviving, renewing (*Brethren, Hang Loose*, pp. 211-214).

I, for one, was unprepared for the extent to which this spiritual restructuring would penetrate my personal life.

As church life changed to follow the biblical pattern, it became apparent that, in order to function within the new forms, personal change would be required on a most basic level. The settings in which we were now seeking to be the church were radically different from what we had been used to. And changed settings began to produce different personal responses. The Spirit and the Word began to speak to issues in our lives which had never before confronted us with such relevance. For example, the relational teachings of Jesus (concerning mutual forgiveness, sharing of goods, servanthood, and commitment to other Christians) began to seem extremely practical and demanded a level of attention more serious than most of us had been giving them.

With developing relationships, increased interaction, and growing confidence in the ministry-capabilities of each other, the level of personal support and accountability intensified. The church became a place to be honest with oneself and to share oneself with others. We talked together about personal matters some of us had never discussed with anyone before. We began to think of growth in terms of personal change more rudimentary than we'd ever dared to consider possible.

> Repentance is fundamental to life in the new society (Mark 1:15). To repent (Greek: *metanoia*) is to be transformed in the basic structures of one's life. Put simply, Jesus' call to enter the kingdom is a call to be changed.
>
> Repentance (choosing to be changed) begins when one turns from independence and self-willful rebellion against God, puts his trust in Jesus Christ, and starts to live with God in relationship rather than alienation. But that's mere beginning. No one is fully changed at that point. He is a new creature in spirit, to be sure. But in mind and life patterns, he is not yet fully renewed. Until a person is related to God, and the Spirit of God lives in him, he does not even see what needs to be changed. And it may take significant time in interaction with Christ's mind for the believer to grasp how extremely vast is the chasm between the alignment of most of his life, and the new mindset toward which he is now being led by the Spirit.
>
> According to Jesus, in Matthew 7:21, living in the kingdom requires obedience to God's will. If we miss the richness of the kingdom in any area of life, it will be

> because we choose to disregard His instructions regarding it. To call Jesus "Lord" is insufficient. The experience of the kingdom is for those who go beyond hearing, knowing, and talking, to *doing* the will of God. In order for this kingdom-constructive pattern to replace the old destructive pattern of the world in every aspect of life, for freedom in Christ's truth to replace the bondage caused by saturation with our godless culture, there must be a continuous bringing of our real lives to the Word of Christ (John 8:31-32), measuring ourselves by it, and adjusting to it . . .
>
> If earth ever sees the kind of community that lives together in the Sermon on the Mount, it will see it emerging among those who repent, who choose to be changed. Discoverers of the kingdom's hidden treasure are those poor in spirit ones, those hungry and thirsty ones who leave the security and comfort of the world's neat systems of value, thought, and living, and place themselves willingly, like a lump of soft clay, in the strong hands of the Potter King. In His hands, everything undergoes change. Everything is reshaped, realigned . . . renewed (*Brethren, Hang Together*, pp. 321-323).

The pursuit of renaissance in our church has resulted in an intensive personal struggle to experience my own personal renewal. It has involved a zealous search for who I really am, what I really believe, and what I am really called and gifted to do. I have struggled to tear away inner emotional hindrances to obedience to Christ. It has been an agonizing campaign calculated to win full healing and freedom for my ministry, my marriage, and my feelings about myself.

This book is designed to provide personal glimpses into this process, and flashes of insight which have come in the heat of the struggle. It is an incomplete, unfinished story—"a slice of the struggle." I hope that people who are being called to be involved in significant change in the church, or who are facing change in their own lives, can identify with it. There are many who are hurting and confused, as I have been all my life in the church, who believe they are alone—no one else, they think, feels what they feel, hurts as they hurt, or has the problems they have.

> Friendship is born at that moment when one person says to another, "What! You too? I thought I was the only one." (C. S. Lewis)

Here is the portrait of a very imperfect Christian. I pray that those who read will see hope, because God's acceptance and love and faithfulness to such a person also comes through.

In the midst of the church's changes I recorded some of the things I was going through, with some of the personal and biblical discoveries that were meaningful to me in the process. At first my writings were scattered, including a few things presented publicly. Later I began to keep a journal, on a hit-or-miss, as-needed basis. This book draws from these two sources. The result: a collection of personal spiritual serendipities growing out of Scripture upon which I was meditating in my times of crisis.

Each chapter combines journal excerpts (which have been edited for publication) and other personal writings, plus current reflections which draw together truths needing emphasis. At Fritz Ridenour's suggestion, *the journal excerpts are set in a different type face from the current reflections*. As you will see on page 19, the chapter begins with my present thoughts. At the bottom of the page, as I tell about "The Stowaway," I am quoting from my journal. I trust that the interaction of past and present will give insight into the renewal process.

—*Robert C. Girard*

My Weakness: His Strength

CHAPTER 1

The Inner Face of Renewal

When I was a child, I talked like a child, I thought like a child, I reasoned like a child. When I became a man, I put childish ways behind me (1 Cor. 13:11).

As the church experienced metamorphosis—gradually changing from the traditional, evangelical form so familiar to most churchgoers, to a strange, new shape more personal and full of surprises—I tumbled out of its broken cocoon, upside down, a naked worm rudely awaking to find myself unprotected, unchanged, and shivering with fear. (More concerning what was involved in the church's "renewal" is told in the *Prologue,* page 11.)

Everything around me had changed, or was in the process of change. Outwardly, in some ways, I looked as if I too had experienced renewal. An interesting new covering was there. And when I fluttered it, it appeared—even to me—as the beginning stages of my very own butterfly wings. But hidden inside, beneath the filmy, half-formed new facade, was the same immature larva which had crawled into the cocoon long ago. Something in my personal process of metamorphosis had gone amuck. Here is how I recorded it in my journal.

The Stowaway

One day in February 1965, about 6:30 in the evening, the Family Girard arrived in Scottsdale, Arizona, from the frozen northland of Minnesota—to begin a new church.

None of us had the vaguest notion that the new church would be as "new" as it eventually became, nor was there any premonition about the vast changes which would be required in my personal philosophy of ministry, my theology, and my relationships. All of these are now substantially different from those of the man I was when we arrived.

Someone came along in the rental truck from Minnesota who has resisted every change. He has been present through all the struggles, joys, and sorrows involved in "renewal." He was there for the first small group meetings which signaled a shift in church direction. He has been there through all the good and bad experiences that have brought us to where we are as a church.

And yet . . . this person has never joined the church!

It seems inconceivable. It is completely baffling to me. But it is true. He has never joined the church as it is today, because he has a basic emotional rigidity about him which makes him unable to accept and adjust to the kind of church which has emerged from the renewal fires. He still clings to a church he knew as a child—the church of his mother.

He is a twelve-year-old boy living in a forty-seven-year-old body. That, apparently, is his main problem. In certain important areas his spiritual and emotional growth seems to have stopped between ages twelve and thirteen. It was about that time he went into hiding . . . behind a veil of suppressed memories.

——— • ———

One of the few things I can remember about my mother is how, nearly every day, she would go into the bathroom, close the door, and pray aloud for her family, one by one, by name. I especially remember hearing her pray for *me*.

I went back to that childhood home in Mobridge, South Dakota. The first time in thirty-four years. Everything had been changed in the house—even doorways and partitions had been moved—*except the bathroom.*

I could still hear her praying.

In the mistiness of memory one feeling lingers at the remembrance of those prayers.

I asked my father last year if he could remember hearing her pray.

Yes, he remembered.

"How did you feel when she prayed?" I asked.

We had both felt one emotion: *guilt.*

In a "healing of the memories" session, I went back (via imagination) to that time and place. And I could hear her praying again her holy, anxious prayers. Asked what I was feeling, I burst into tears. Asked what I wanted to do, I said, "I want to say, 'Mama! Don't worry about me. I'm okay. See, I grew up to be a good boy. Please, Mama! Please think I'm a good boy.'"

Mama was a devout Christian whose outward life was probably *too* perfect, in that it masked the human weakness within. She taught her children by precept and example to respond to the authority of the church, with respect and receptiveness. It was only natural, then, for a sensitive child to adopt the picture of God presented by the authority figures of the church (i.e., teachers, pastors, evangelists). These people, many of whom I loved dearly, presented the clearest and best picture they had to share—even though it was a picture of God which was woefully, destructively lacking.

The God they focalized—and I as a boy believed in—was a God who seemed to offer love only in exchange for performance—*perfect* performance of all of the biblical commands.

God of Anger

Through no intent to deceive, God was presented as one who relentlessly punishes sin and sinners with impartial and blood-curdling vengeance. God was said to be merciful to *repenting sinners*—vastly forgiving of all misdeeds committed by non-Christians—but impatient with believers who fall into sin. A Christian "does not commit sin." If he does, he cannot be a Christian.

Early memorization and repetition of John 3:16's "For God so loved . . ." was never enough to drown out the heavy emphasis on the wrath and judgment of a God angry with sin, whose love was severely limited by "ifs." In complete justice and consistency this God could withdraw His love and acceptance at the slightest failure to achieve spiritual, moral, and emotional perfection. Thus, one moment a person could be a child of God; the next moment—because of some willful sin of word, thought, deed, or omission—he could again find himself a child of wrath.

The "mourner's bench" in front of the church was stained by my childish tears of repentance again and again and again. But every determined effort to produce the kind of perfect behavior that could please God (and nothing short of perfection—as the church and Mama defined and demonstrated it—could ever please Him) ended in failure and increasing guilt and despair in the deepening conviction that *I would never make it!* If I had not been so terrified of going to hell I might have given up my efforts to be saved. But I kept hoping that some day I too would enter into that "full" spiritual experience (the one the authority figures all claimed) which would, at last, set me free to live the life of Christian perfection and thus satisfy God.

I cannot recall a single incident in which one of my spiritual mentors ever shared that he too had spiritual struggles, was sometimes weak, and sometimes failed to win against sin in his life. They had all, apparently, "come into the experience." So, I was left with the dreadful feeling that I, alone, was the only one for whom pleasing God was impossible! I was so weak, such a bad person, that I could not be saved!

To further confuse the issue, I was taught that God demanded that I love him and believe in Him—no matter what He might do; that I be willing to lay down my life for others, with uninterrupted love and sweetness—regardless of anything they might do to me. But if I was weak enough to fall short of even one of His instructions, He summarily pronounced my condemnation and threatened me with everlasting fire.

What a frustrating God! How grossly unfair! Such a God should not be surprised if I burn with anger toward Him!

When Mama died of leukemia (an "incurable disease of the blood," they called it), I was twelve. After her death my loneliness was so intense as to be beyond expression. I was afraid it was *my sin* that had led to her death! (Thirty-four years later, my dad confessed to me that he had secretly taken on the same guilt, and for three and a half decades has feared that *his sins* were responsible for her death—that his wife's terminal illness was punishment from God!)

The Hiding Place

A year later, Daddy remarried. The fresh and painful memory of Mama haunted the new marriage and led to inevitable comparisons and conflcts in the family. To deal with this extremely difficult situation, the subject of Mama was made a family "taboo." It was an unwise and unhealthy decision, but at the time seemed necessary to bring peace to the home.

And so . . . stopped short in the midst of the grieving process, unable to complete it in a normal way, forced into premature silence about the deepest agony of my young life, I hunted for ways to escape the pain of feelings I was no longer at liberty to express.

Without understanding what I was doing, at thirteen years, I began to systematically force my deepest feelings of grief and guilt—along with a host of painful questions about life and death and God and mother—out of conscious thought, and deep into the darkness of my subconscious mind.

It was as though, at that point, the hurting child I was went into hiding. Most early memories were pushed beyond the point of recall. Mama became a shadowy figure tinged with scarcely recognizable feeling tones.

Child of Anger

The child did not die. There in his dark inner cell, he has continued to cry and hurt and fear, and to nurse unexpressable anger. That anger has often exploded from the vault of darkness with surprising ferocity and destructiveness, leaving both me and those near me baffled as to where it came from.

As a man, I have been capable of some rather demanding commitments: marriage, fathering three children, full-time pastoral ministry. Some people think of me as a spiritual leader, a man of God. As a man, I have been conceptually converted to the real God revealed in Jesus Christ—the True God, whose personal attitudes are accurately reflected in the personality of Jesus. I have reached a rather mature intellectual understanding of God.

And yet, there has been this clandestine part of me which has not, until recently, been brought face to face with the God of love and grace and the Christian life of forgiveness and freedom. My "feeling child" apparently still believes the theology of my mother's church. For in spite of the growth that has come in my adult experience with God, inside I still deal with an emotional waif whose most dominant personal characteristics are:

Fear .... of rejection, failure, or disapproval by people and by God.

Guilt .... generated by failure to achieve perfection, triggered by criticism or by any hint of personal non-acceptance.

Perfectionism .... which results in painful dissatisfaction with nearly everything I do, often drives me to work and worry when it's time to play and rest, and gives birth to judgmental attitudes toward the imperfections of others.

Sensitivity .... which is defensive, easily hurt by criticism and deeply wounded by rejection, and thus sometimes finds forgiveness difficult.

Rigidity .... a self-protective inflexibility which resists change and magnifies disappointments all out of proportion.

Confusion .... over love, sexuality and personal acceptability, which leads to great pain in making decisions.

Anger .... I am learning to cry when I'm hurt, but the most "natural" response, the one with which I am most comfortable, is to become angry.

Anger may be the more dominant characteristic of this "buried-alive" emotional child. A recent personality inventory disclosed that inside (in the child's hiding place) is a lifetime supply of "stored up" hostility. As light has been brought in, it has been discovered that most of this cache of unexpressed aggression is directed toward God—the God who will not allow the slightest imperfection without withdrawing His love—the God who, as punishment for childhood sins, would take away a boy's mother at the time he most needs her—the unreasonable God who continually withholds strength to live the perfect life He demands—the God who would never forgive until begged publicly before the whole church!

It has been maddening to have such a perception of God! It has been impossible to please Him. I have always been in trouble with Him. But nothing could be more unthinkable than to *feel anger* toward a God who will send a person "straight to hell" for a single sin! I did not dare to yell at this God. So I learned to bury my anger. But, sadly, anger is never dealt with by interment. It continues to seethe below the level of consciousness like a buried land mine awaiting pressure from some unsuspecting victim who may happen to step on the wrong spot. Almost any reversal, rejection, problem, criticism, failure, fear, or other painful or threatening experience becomes a fuse to ignite such a stockpile of unexpressed aggression. Seldom in my life has it blown Godward. Mostly it has blasted away at my baffled wife and family.

The Child and the Ministry

It is highly possible—even probable—that a major motivation for my entrance into the ecclesiastical ministry as a full-time vocation was this clinging, heretofore unsuccessful childish drive to please my mother and her God. Once embarked on that course, still fearful of His (and her) frown, I consumed my energies in what I can now admit has been a desperate striving for success and acceptance.

I pursued the madness of trying to prove my worth by leading the churches I pastored toward statistical success —because it would almost surely draw approval from "the people who count"—at the high cost of neglected relationships and unattended priorities. Tragically, what achievements there were, invariably were robbed of the joy they should have held for me by their unrelenting imperfectness. When I honestly faced my successes, I was painfully reminded by a neurotic conscience that *they could never possibly be good enough to make up for my failures!*

The load of "pastoral expectations" (i.e., the expectations of people and what I supposed were the expectations of God) has been overwhelming to my fragile ego. It has repeatedly filled me with guilt and rage. More disastrous, it has moved me to mismanage, for most of my ministerial life, many God-given personal priorities, deep and holy personal desires, valuable personal gifts and ministry dreams, in order to meet the expectations of church boards, self-motivated parishioners, a tradition-bound denomination, and even the secular community. I am seeing it now unmasked as a widely-accepted form of ministerial *prostitution.*

Somehow, in spite of my fears and neurotic obsession with success, I dared to dream of radical change in the church. As I recall, it was at a point of dismal failure in my ministry, when I was feeling bad enough, inadequate enough, to actually listen when the Holy Spirit began to reveal to me some of the forgotten principles of church life visible in the New Testament church. So much that I had never experienced seemed to be promised there. I was keenly aware of personal needs that biblical church-life could probably be serving—needs the church, as we were then, was not even beginning to touch.

When renewal began for our local congregation, I was in it up to my ears! Its leading exponent. I felt inspired with hope, exhilarated with the adventure of spiritual renaissance. I could see beyond the struggles, reverses, tensions, and attritions to "the glory that will be revealed in us." The *man* I am fully joined the "new" church, applauded its uniqueness, and was welcomed by it with open arms.

But through the entire restructuring process, the feeling child in me has remained rigid, suffering extreme discomfort with the changes happening around him. This part of me has reacted as if Christ never came. Interiorly, each alteration in the church's lifestyle gave rise to spasms of fear that God would not be pleased, and would punish me for making wrong or stupid choices. Whenever anyone became disillusioned with what was happening in the life of the spiritual community and decided to leave—and there were many of these—inside me burned a deep sense of personal failure, worthlessness, and rejection. Often snarling hostility would erupt to the surface—anger that God would seem to lead us so clearly to take the steps toward change, and then would fail to bless our faith with the kind of success which could convince us, and the skeptics watching us, that we were right.

I resented deeply the crushing sense of responsibility—lonely responsibility—for the success or failure, not only of myself, but of the entire church. It seemed to me that I carried on my head all the embarrassment, defeat, uncertainty, rejection, failure, and anxiety—and judgment—of the whole church and everyone in it!

The emotionally, theologically stunted boy in me is driven to produce in order to be accepted, and must succeed in the eyes of his peers in order to prove his worth. He is trapped in a whirlpool of unhealed self-doubt, and enslaved to an outdated covenant, an unbiblical picture of God and the church. He needs very badly to be saved, set free from these destructive misconceptions. However, salvaton must reach more than his intellect, which is already quite soundly converted. Deliverance and regeneration must penetrate the depths of the buried child, still crying from the misty caverns of the subconscious mind. Because out of those shadowy deeps come many of the patterns of response which still dominate important areas of my life.

The clandestine child needs to know God knows and accepts and loves him, as he is. Like all twelve-year-olds, once exposed, he will probably turn out to be not a bad sort at all. Like a typical subteen, he is at times frustrating, uninformed, and inept. But if he can simply breathe the free air of grace and light, perhaps, in time, he can become free to play again, laugh with abandon, love without fear, genuinely enjoy being alive, and approve of newness in the church. Who knows? He may have the hidden potential for leading the whole congregation in the dance of joy!

We will no longer be infants, tossed back and forth by the waves, and blown here and there by every wind of teaching and by the cunning and craftiness of men in their deceitful scheming. Instead, speaking the truth in love, we will in all things grow up into him who is the Head, that is, Christ (Eph. 4:14–15).

CHAPTER 2

The Dawning of Righteousness

If we walk in the light, as he is in the light, we have fellowship with one another, and the blood of Jesus, his son, purifies us from every sin (1 John 1:7).

On the last day of January I went to Yuma for a special visit with my father. In my hand I carried three legal-sized pages of questions I intended to ask—questions neither of us had talked about for thirty-four years.

It was the beginning of a walk with Jesus back into my all-but-forgotten childhood to uncover the roots of spiritual problems which have persisted through a third-of-a-century of my life as a Christian.

For eight hours we engaged in memory-freeing conversation. I came away loving him more than ever. And understanding both of us better than ever. So much of those childhood years had been blocked from memory, but as he told the stories, memory revived—I actually was able to remember them myself. I had gone to him with three pages of questions; I returned with . . . my childhood.

On the 185-mile trip home, I talked with my Heavenly Father about the new/old revelations I had just been given. There was a refreshing sense that, at last, the hidden things of my life were being exposed to God's light. I found myself anticipating inner healing. I began to visualize the Father cleansing and curing stubborn spiritual diseases which have sprung from ancient, secret roots. Now that the secrets were out, I could start, specifically, to trust God with the early happenings of my life, consciously surrendering them, one by one, to Him.

As I made homeward tracks, the New Testament's message concerning *light* came to mind. Traveling down the interstate at fifty-five miles per hour, I opened my Bible and read and praised and shouted and sang and confessed my way through First John 1—for three hours.

First John 1 has become a how-to booklet for taking newly exposed memories to the Father and going through the great spiritual transactions. Old unresolved fears, hostilities, guilts, and griefs have begun to yield to the touch of His loving-kindness. Faith has never reached so deep. An urgency has attached itself to the continuing task of bringing myself fully into the light, with my unburied past as well as the details of my present life.

Dawn Versus Dark

An excursion back into childhood is not a prerequisite to experiencing God's grace. However, the Bible clearly states that there are some things offered us in His gracious plan, there are heights of fellowship and holiness, which elude us to the extent that we live with ourselves, one another, and God in darkness rather than light.

The pivotal concept of First John 1 is "God is light" (v. 5).

In this declaration, the apostle is not being carried away with lofty flights into poetic fuzziness. Nor is he mouthing a mere mentally adopted theological proposition. "God is light" is, to John, solid reality. With the other apostles, he has had a real-life experience with the God who is light. He describes it with words such as "heard" (three times), "seen" (three times), "appeared" (twice), "looked at," "touched," and so on—courtroom words describing hard evidence (John 1).

The unseen Father of all life has disclosed Himself in Jesus. God has come out into the open and clearly trusted himself to the senses—the eyes, ears, touch, and perceptions—of people (vv. 1–3). His self-disclosure is complete and personal and intimate. The word *koinonia* is used to describe it (v. 3, "fellowship"). It means sharing, interaction, communication, community, "sharing the common life."[1] In Jesus, God comes close enough for us to experience *family* with Him. To encounter God as light is to know the inner reality of personal intercourse with the Father and the Son.

In God's example we discover that walking in "light" involves self-disclosure, sharing reality on a personal level, leading to intimacy.

The antithesis of light is "darkness."

Darkness (*skotas*) is gloom, blindness, obscurity, shadiness, shroudedness, and secrecy or privacy (Matt. 10:27, Luke 12:3). First John 1:6 (NASB) states that the "walk in darkness" involves lying and failure to "practice the truth." Light's antithesis embraces falsehood, deceit, dishonesty, hypocrisy, cover-up, denial, opaqueness, manipulation—any form of not telling or living or facing the truth. None of these things characterizes God. "In Him there is no darkness at all" (v. 5).

The genuineness and intimacy of our fellowship with God (v. 6) and with one another (v. 7) depends on the extent to which we "walk in the light" instead of the dark, and "practice the truth" instead of dishonesty.

The contrast in the two lifestyles comes into focus in the conversation Jesus has with Nicodemus in John 3. This overheard conversation may have been John's first exposure to the concepts "practice the truth" and "walk in the light." Here is the gist of it (vv. 16–21).

Just judgment is based on consideration of solid evidence. Jesus, God as light, came into the world, not to condemn, but to save. But His presence here—the light shining in the dark (John 1:5)—judged the world. For, wherever He went, whatever He did, all He was, left a trail, not only of saved people, but of unmasked rebellion.

Wherever He went, there were those who believed God's love-gift and came to the light, even though it meant exposure of their personal sinfulness, spiritual poverty, and lostness. But there were others who hated the same light, because of this very exposure, and utterly rejected its findings in their lives. These chose spiritual dishonesty. They did not welcome the light. But it was too late. Light had come. Their sin and poverty had been uncovered. They stood condemned by their choice to close off to light and to go on living a lie.

> But he who practices the truth comes to the light, that his deeds may be manifested as having been wrought in God (John 3:21 NASB).

Followers of Jesus are those who choose to live in God's own broad-daylight style. They choose to allow God's own character to expose them for what they really are, with all that involves of uncovering sin and exposing deceit. They choose to live in truthfulness about themselves and openness about what is going on in their lives. They are called to a lifestyle of being known—a "no-darkness lifestyle"—which affects the way they relate to one another and how they deal with the realities of their own lives.

Christians sometimes fear the process of introspection. They sometimes exhort one another to the effect that it is neither healthy nor spiritual to look deeply within. And there may be some danger in exposing interior reality if one pursues the search alone, without the Holy Spirit and the Word of God and support of fellow believers. If one looks only to himself for resources with which to deal with the issues he unmasks, he risks devastating failure and suicidal hopelessness. Having admitted that, I must hasten to add that without some facing of one's inner poverty, one is unlikely to understand his need for help, his need for God, and, as a Christian, his need for growth.

Jesus persists in urging the cleansing of "the inside of the cup," the inner treasure of the heart, the inner abundance out of which the mouth speaks. What defiles a person, he insists, is the surfacing of what is inside (Matt. 23:25–26, 12:34–35, Mark 7:20–21). He declares that a person's inner sinful desires are tantamount to the actual sinful deed (Matt. 5:28). He calls disciples into a lifestyle so selfless and to attitudes so pure that I, for one, cannot begin to respond without an inner purging which clears away specific subconscious spiritual barriers. For there are "automatic" response mechanisms in me which leap into action when the right situational button is punched. I have "instinctive" fears, prejudices, and blind spots. My subconscious mind employs secret techniques to evade the real issues. All these covert dynamics are destructive and must be dealt with in the light.

A healthy, purposeful self-examination, guided by the Word, energized by the Holy Spirit and supported by "caring others," is often necessary. David unashamedly prayed,

> Search me, O God, and know my heart; Try me and know my anxious thoughts; And see if there be any hurtful way in me, And lead me in the everlasting way. (Ps. 139:23–24 NASB)

Once the inner patterns become visible, I may move to make God's evaluation of them my own. And, with expanded understanding, I can bring myself and my discoveries to Him in knowing relinquishment. There is a sense in which I cannot "agree with God" (confess) if I do not know something of the realities of who and what I am, or if I am in the dark about what He thinks about those realities.

We are assured that in Christ there is no condemnation (Rom. 8:1)—He accepts us as we are, forgives and covers our sin at this very moment, and patiently suffers the vast areas of our ignorance. But there are aspects of the purification process which wait for *willing* exposure to the light. Free from condemnation, we need not fear to be known.

Light and Healing

A further effect of the transparent lifestyle is pinpointed in James 5:16. The Lord's brother affirms the vital link between being known and being healed:

> Confess your sins to each other and pray for each other so that you may be healed.

Healing from sin's destructive effects is one of the accomplishments of Christ's atonement (Isa. 53:5). More than once, Jesus linked deliverance from sin with healing (i.e., the case of the paralytic brought by friends, who was assured of forgiveness of his sins as a prelude to his physical healing, Matt. 9:1–8; the case of the man at the pool who, upon being restored to health, was warned to sin no more lest a worse malady befall him, John 5:14).

Modern medicine understands that the subconscious mind is capable of projecting guilt for unforgiven sin, a sense of unworthiness, undealt-with hostility, or some other intense negative emotion, on some part of the body, until actual physical disease symptoms appear. No healing that purports to be complete dare ignore the guilt or other unresolved inner conflict behind the illness.

Physical healing often hinges on allowing ourselves to be known to our fellow Christians, so that they can pray powerful prayers for us from positions of understanding. Until there is a conscious, purposeful "coming into the light," many kinds of emotional, spiritual, physical, and relational restoration cannot come. Personal honesty and self-disclosure—exposure of sin-conditioned inner structures to the light—are part of an effective biblical approach to healing and change.

Stepping Into the Light

I have decided that I am going to live more openly, more honestly with God and the people in my life.

I have been lonely long enough. I want the depth of fellowship promised in the light.

Long enough I have been plagued by these old, destructive, sinful spiritual and emotional patterns. If honesty before God and the people around me, open confession, knowing and facing myself and who I am, are keys to cleansed and healed response-mechanisms, leading to more complete obedience, I'm awfully hungry for it. And I intend to pursue it with vigor.

I'm hungry enough now to respond to God's own example of reaching out to build intimacy with us. I'm hungry enough to be (like Him) available to be heard, seen, touched, and disclosed in truthfulness and reality. I want the people in my life to know me.

The promises of forgiveness, cleansing, joy, and the manifest working of God in me are just too good to pass up! (1 John 1:4, 7, 9; John 3:21).

Not long before the commencement of my fourteenth year as pastor at Our Heritage Church, I had an unexpected encounter with God, in which His light probed surprisingly deep into unilluminated areas of my life.

At an informal, spontaneous home meeting, I was given an insight which rocked me back on my heels. I realized that imbedded in my personality on the level of my "automatic" emotional responses were deep and rigid barriers to full obedience to Christ. It came as a sense of sin deeper than I had ever experienced before.

I saw that sin had set its patterns so deeply in my person, that, as much as I wished to respond to all that Jesus taught, I simply could not. For example, I could talk of living without lust (Matt. 5:28), but I could not do it. I could talk of turning the other cheek (Matt. 5:39–41), and of loving my enemies (Matt. 5:43–47), but when under attack I instinctively responded with fear leading to anger and resentment, which, if not expressed outwardly toward the attacker, rose up at some unexpected place to wreak its destruction. I could talk of forgiveness and reconciliation (Matt. 5:23–24, 18:21–22) and could even go through the motions of forgiving, but upon meeting or thinking about those who had rejected me, I was flooded anew with fear and resentment. I could talk of caring nothing for material things (Matt. 6:25–33) and of freely giving (Matt. 5:42, Luke 6:30–36), but the thought of sharing my resources frightened me. So I either clung tightly to my things or too-cautiously meted out my sharing almost to the point of stinginess. I could talk of love (John 13:34–35) and of laying down my life for my friends (John 15:12–13), but I found within myself an unexplained resistance to developing close relationships, to giving myself to others, and to putting others before myself without pride or resentment. I could recite the Beatitudes (Matt. 5:3–10), preach from them, tell others how to have such attitudes, but my "automatic" inner responses were more often exactly the opposite to these "basics of the kingdom lifestyle."

Fear stood in the way of obedience at most points. Fear I could not make go away by "simply trusting."

To compound the matter, I discovered I had become a master of rationalization, projection, and denial. I had a "reasonable explanation" for most of my failures to obey. Often, my explanation involved unconsciously projecting my own reluctance and rebellion onto other people:

"I cannot do what I feel God wants me to do, because of his/her prejudice, hang-up, or blindness."

"He/she would really give me trouble if I did what Jesus says."

So . . . "It's his/her fault, not mine, that I cannot follow Christ more perfectly."

When I saw the truth about these things, I wept and confessed my spiritual undoneness before my friends. I did not know where to start to bring about the inner deliverance and change needed. I simply realized that there was much about myself I did not know, and therefore did not understand how to surrender to God. But I agreed with God that deep inner healing was needed, and that I would seek it.

At that point my inner search became specific. In addition to abundant interaction with my spouse and other spiritual kin—interaction aimed at self-discovery and resolution of personal spiritual deficiencies being uncovered by the Spirit—I joined a "Yokefellow" group. After the first group ended, I joined a second. The Yokefellow program (as we have experienced it) involves commiting oneself to a small group of people who come together weekly over an extended period of months to discuss their emotional/spiritual weaknesses, to help each understand himself better, to encourage one another, to take steps toward positive change and growth, to pray for and with one another, and to stimulate each to present himself in more complete surrender to God. The group becomes both the setting for self-revelation and mutual acceptance and the catalyst for change.

On this journey, the results of three "spiritual growth inventories" (taken as part of the Yokefellow experience) were effective in the Holy Spirit's hands to cut through my spiritual blindness and reveal the specific nature of my inner spiritual barriers. For example, though I have been in the church since birth, the Christian ministry has consumed the last twenty-seven years of my life and I have written two published books on the subject of church renewal. One of these "inventories," unimpressed by my record, exhumed the buried truth that I am, on the feeling level, a captive of tradition. Intellectually I am a thoroughly orthodox Christian, committed to the renaissance of the church. My "emotional philosophy of life," however, is not the joy-filled realism of Jesus, but a personal "religion" of doubt, fear, negativism, and materialism! Though with my conscious mind and my mouth I have loudly denied it. While, by now, I should have learned to love myself and others with some liberty, and should have developed a healthy inner flexibility, the personality inventory showed me to be, in many ways, not what my belief-system mandates, but just the opposite: basically selfish, often resentful, and fiercely rigid. Many of the concepts I believe and preach have not, evidently, taken deep root in my subconscious mind, where the circuits which control my primal emotional responses are activated.

It is not hard to admit, now that it has been lighted up. I realize that I have known all along. But with the light shining in that dark closet, I can no longer ignore its disarray. The tough issues raised must be confronted. The spiritual transactions needed must be pursued. The growth demanded must be cultivated. I cannot remain the same—I've seen the light! Faith must be activated on the level of the emotions and affections that move my life and control my behavior.

In other ways, I have sought the intrusion of light. A trip to dimly-remembered important childhood places in South Dakota put me in touch with forgotten-but-not-dead feelings, unspoken-yet-unresolved griefs and guilts. At strategic points in the process I have sought the insights of trusted fellow Christians who are trained and/or gifted in personal counselling. They have helped me understand the changes taking place and the revelations coming to light. One led me through a process of "inner healing." I'll describe it later.

Further, I have run to the Word repeatedly, to dig for pure glimpses of the thinking of God about who I am and what I am experiencing.

In all this scrambling for light, my goals have been (1) to know myself, to understand who I am, why I am like I am, and what in me still needs healing and liberating in order for me to become what God created me and called me to be; (2) to be enabled to bring myself to God in fuller, more perceptive surrender; (3) to be healed of destructive emotional habits that are disrupting my life and sand-bagging my responsiveness to God; (4) to learn how to hear the voice of God above the other voices which seek to shape my attitudes and choices; (5) to be inwardly freed to obey Christ in all that He has taught, and (6) to be changed more and more into the likeness of Jesus.

Transparency and Modeling

Transparency is foundational to discipling people and to developing the kind of church that is responsive to God's process of changing us into His Son's likeness. But there are people who become extremely uncomfortable when "the man of God" begins to share the realities of his personal struggle. The mere suggestion that, in some areas of his life, he is not the paragon of spiritual power and godly virtue they have dreamed he was, is enough to send waves of shock through a congregation.

One woman would not accept my passing public statement that I too sometimes have problems with lust. She saw immediately my identification with the sins of her unfaithful husband! And it was a true identification. My occasional lust, though it has not led me into unfaithfulness to my wife, *is* the same sin he has acted out.

One older man who loved me dearly shook his hoary head in disbelief when I shared my struggle with anger. He simply could not accept the truth.

Some people lose "respect" when a leading brother unveils his face. But what is lost is a respect based on a *false image.* Others, in my experience, began to respect me more deeply when I removed the veil. (See 2 Cor. 3:12, 17–18.)

In either case, it seemed essential that I take the risk. I wanted the power available through true identification with people. I wanted to be able to say, "Follow me as I follow Christ!" and then *show the way* in dealing with personal struggles and sins, by letting people go through my spiritual transactions with me. I also hoped that the identification and way-showing would be *mutual*—that at last I might have some help for my own areas of defeat.

I wanted something I had never been sure of before. I desired to know the satisfaction of *true* respect—respect for the person I really am in Christ, rather than the empty gratification of respect based on remaining *unknown*!

Becoming transparent makes one vulnerable to misunderstanding and suffering. But there is no way to model how a believer works through problems, weaknesses, and failures unless one is known well enough over a long enough time to be observed dealing with his struggles and defeats as well as his victories.

> For you who fear My name the sun of righteousness will rise with healing in its wings; and you will go forth and skip about like calves from the stall (Mal. 4:2).

CHAPTER 3

The Weaning

*Surely I have composed and quieted my soul;
Like a weaned child rests against his mother,
My soul is like a weaned child within me
(Ps. 131:2 NASB).*

Weaning and Growing

There is no true maturity without weaning.

The babe is removed from the breast to learn to live free from its mother, and to grow strong on solid food and independent life-shaping experiences. The youth is encouraged to leave the home-nest, to be his/her own person, to learn to live responsibly, to grow to be the kind of person on whom others may depend.

In sound discipling, the spiritual "elder" serves his "younger" to bring him to where, "graduated" from his discipler, he knows God for himself, is able to hear the voice of the Holy Spirit for his own life, and is able to initiate and carry out his own life-ministry. As he grows and is freed, a mutual style of discipling replaces the elder-younger style.

Ministry and church life (like raising healthy children) should be structured in such a way that those in its care are led out of babyhood into the kind of spiritual adulthood, liberty, and sensitivity that equips them to feed, challenge, and renew even the practitioners and structures which helped to nurture them.

This pattern is modeled in the ways of God with His children. The Old Testament Law was given, circumscribing every particular of their lives within the written code. Later, in Christ, God weaned them from the Law, setting them free to live in response to the voice of the Holy Spirit (Rom. 7:6).

Jesus brought the Twelve into the firm, secure confinement of face-to-face interaction with Him. Later, according to plan, He weaned them from their dependence on the visible and sent them out in the same way the Father had sent Him out (John 20:21-23).

The Jerusalem congregation clung daily to the apostles' teaching and might have continued thus 'til the Lord's return (Acts 2:42). At the right moment, however, the "gift" of Saul's violent persecution facilitated their weaning. Freed from the security of their first teachers, they scurried in all directions, preaching and doing the Good News wherever they ran (Acts 8:1-4).

Paul and Barnabas nestled snugly and grew up spiritually among the Christians at Antioch. When it was time, the Holy Spirit spoke to their comrades and the two were pushed out of the cozy spiritual nest and into an expanded ministry (Acts 13:1-3).

The apostles founded churches of those who believed their message. The young Christian communities shed torrents of tears when, after only a few months of ministry, their spiritual fathers left them alone and expected them to be the church *all by themselves*—without the help of their founders (Acts 14:23).

In time, the weaning must always come, or the growth and maturity will not.

All our personal relationships, including our relationship with God, can and should be growing through and beyond the stage of *dependence,* in which those relationships are held together purely on the basis of need and expectation. Healthy growth can free us to value the persons in our lives for their own sakes. "Being fed" must ultimately cease to be the chief motive for loving and relating. The wholeness and joy of *interdependency* hinges on such growth.

Weaning is a necessary part of the process of becoming catalysts rather than merely "defenders of the status quo."

Mothers and Substitutes

I am in the process of being weaned.

When I was an infant, my mother fed me at her breasts. When I was less than a year old, she transferred me to the bottle—a substitute for mother's personal feeding. Later, by whatever process, I was weaned from the bottle too. I do not remember if it was traumatic. Chances are, it was.

But necessary.

When I was twelve, my mother on whom I depended, died. I felt more alone and separated than anyone really understood. I was sure I could not survive without her. But she was gone.

So . . . unconsciously, I began to seek for someone to mother me.

My first substitute mother was the church. The church that had been so important to my mother became my place of security and comfort. I clung to her and fed my emotional needs at her breast. My whole concept of selfhood became deeply entwined with the institutional church. At age fifteen, I enrolled (of my own choice) at a denominationally-operated boarding school, where I was "adopted" and "bottle fed" by a tiny, loving religious community. My *alma mater* became, literally, "fostering mother."

Considering the intensity of the emotional attachment I entered into with the institutional, denominational church, it was predictable that I would enter "the ministry." The heroes of campus and community were the "theologs"—those God-touched young martyrs-in-training who would "give all" for their fostering mother. In my fervid desire to please her, I answered the call to full-time Christian service. Whether or not I was, at the same time, genuinely responding to the voice of God is a question presently demanding an answer. I suspect I will discover that the answer is yes. But it seems clear that the shape of my response was set more by the institution than by the mind of God.

As our local congregation and I have moved toward renewal during the decade just past, many changes have been required in church structure and priorities. Very little is left which fits the denominational/institutional norm. Nothing is done "by the book" any more. This has set in motion one of my life's most painful conflicts. For, while it is true that I have purposely resisted and abandoned many of the historic "parental" traditions of the institution, it is nonetheless true that I have wanted nothing more than to please her. Through it all, I have continued to anticipate maternal affirmation and approval from my dear substitute. But since the denomination can never approve of me and my work, I am left pining for favor and acceptance from a fostering mother who I know full well can never give it

———— • ————

Lord, how am I to respond to this unweaned yearning for a mother's approval? How can I convince the longing child in me that Mama is dead and her approval or disapproval need have nothing more to do with my sense of personal value?

———— • ————

The mother of my childhood may not have understood or approved a church so unlike her beloved church. Perhaps she would spank me with a wire clothes hanger for my nonconforming naughtiness, as when I was a boy. But she is with Jesus now, and she knows as she is known, sees face to face, is more alive to the kingdom value system than I am. If Jesus approves of us. . . . because she is like Him now, Mama approves.

What matters, in the final analysis, is the approval of Jesus. I may be as wrong as my denominational leaders think I am. My church may be failing to be all a church ought to be. But He knows our faith. He knows that in our weak, wobbly, childlike way, the church and I are honestly trying to respond to Him.

———— • ————

Get it through to me, Lord. So I can stand the pain when misunderstanding and rejection come. It is no longer important what Mama would have thought or what my substitute mother thinks. Let it be enough to be accepted and approved by You!

It is time to stop clinging to the institutional church as a source of security, affirmation, and nurture. (If she gives support, praise God. If she withholds it, praise Him no less.) I have grown up and no longer need that surrogate supplier of infant wants. My dependence on her must be left among the "childish things" with which the mature do away (1 Cor. 13:11). She is, after all, about to cast me out, disinherit me—amid accusations that I have forsaken her. It is foolish to continue to clamor for her comforts. It is time for "the right sort of independence" from her (James 1:4, Phillips). Her paps are dry. She no longer embraces me when I beg for her affection. To keep begging, returning to those dried up nipples is to continually set up the mechanics of rejection.

It's weaning time, little boy.

The Mother-Son Syndrome

My search for a mother did not end in the institutional church. And my weaning touches more than my ecclesiastical relationships.

While being nurtured in the bosom of the church, I met and loved and married Audrey. She was a delightful companion, with attractive qualities that were rare and deep and she added important elements to my life. She would be a "good preacher's wife." (That would please my mother.)

It has been a good marriage built on a "till death do us part" commitment. We have been best friends and confidants through the years. We have been at each other's side, holding hands, time and time again when the chips were down. Neither of us has wanted to do anything important without the other—whether a vacation, a conferred honor, a tough battle, a major decision, a new career, or a spiritual discovery. We believed that marriage was two becoming one, and we have tried to make that work. We have nurtured, comforted, challenged, and served each other, as we have understood the need, and according to our personal resources. We have loved each other and said it often. We have enjoyed a healthy physical love-life, and have found great delight in each other's arms.

We have fought some healthy battles—and some destructive ones. We have been hurt and we have been wrong. But we have never withdrawn into isolation for long. We have not always been skillful in expressing our true feelings, but somehow we found ways to talk about them. We have failed at communication often, but never for lack of trying.

The marriage survived some years of neglect—when I was too busy to give it the attention it needed. But in recent years, I have been willing even to cancel important appointments at the last minute to deal with the needs of our relationship.

However, one aspect of the relationship between Audrey and me has been a major source of conflict and pain. It has been with us from honeymoon days. For many years we were quite baffled by it. It has often left us frustrated, angry, and dissatisfied. But lately, we have been dragging it out into the light, and together, with dogged determination and, at times, crusading zeal, have proceeded to attack it as though the future of our marriage depends on how we deal with this issue.

We have dubbed this subtle, destructive force, "the mother-son syndrome."

Through the first eighteen years of marriage we tried to talk it through, pray it away, and cover it over with forgiveness. But despite all our efforts the pattern persisted. Again and again fear or frustration would trigger extremely painful "arguments." They were marked, on my part, by outbursts of rage, which exploded in destructive fury in response to my feeling (I had not so well identified it at the time) that I was in danger of being "controlled," or that I was being treated like a naughty child. My reaction to questioning (about anything), protectiveness, correction, or disagreement was often like a child whose mother is calling it to account.

After one such painful scenario Audrey began to ask God specifically for some sort of revelation on what the real problem between us was. I do not remember how long she prayed and read and researched (perhaps several months). But the day came when she knew God had spoken. And I agreed.

We began at that point to wrestle with what was immediately apparent to both of us, once its wraps were removed. A major barrier to the health of our marriage lay in the fact that, without understanding what we were doing or the developmental reasons behind it, we had fallen quite "naturally" into the *wrong roles* in certain component aspects of our life together. Audrey, with her strong natural maternal instincts, almost "automatically" assumed the mother-role at times. I, drawn just as "automatically" into the role by my unfulfilled emotional needs, have played the child in those scenes.

> It seems apparent that with all the other things I had been looking for and found in Audrey during our courtship, there was part of me that was, unconsciously, still engaged in a childish search for a substitute mother!
>
> In many areas we have done a good job as husband and wife. For the most part, I have carried my responsibility as leader, provider, and lover. Generally, Audrey has been responsive, adapting herself to me, my personality, my dreams, and my call, honoring me as family leader.
>
> I have "fed at her breasts" for the right reasons: for romance, marital intimacy, the joy of sexual love-making. But in another sense—a thoughtlessly immature and selfish sense—I have sought her maternal feeding for purely neurotic reasons. I have clamored and begged and manipulated her to fill my infantile hunger for approval and affirmation. I have leaned too heavily on her for my sense of security and worth. Conflicts have been the inevitable result, because she could not always respond to my crying. Her own needs cried out to be met too.
>
> The "little boy" who came along in the package with the man who said, "I do," came into marriage with secret emotional deficiencies. To this inner child, all external approval is merely an inadequate and frustrating "band-aid" applied to a self-image whose wounds require corrective surgery. But without any such clear diagnosis of the problem, I kept returning to Audrey's bosom, seeking more than anyone responding alone could consistently give. Our relationship has been plagued again and again by unreasonable and demanding expectations which neither of us could fulfill. Hence, the erosion of the simple enjoyment of being together as lovers and friends.

For the last nine of our twenty-seven married years we have been consciously confronting this syndrome in order to bring fuller health into our husband-wife relationship. It has been a painful struggle for both of us. *A lot like weaning for me.* Weaning! After more than forty years of begging for a return to the breast, and being dissatisfied with the substitutes!

Our approach to dealing with this "mother-son thing" has been simple. (Note: I did not say *easy.*)

1. We have talked about it at great length. We have looked for the underlying causes of the automatic ease with which we fall into this destructive pattern (i.e., my unconscious "substitute mother search" and self-image deficiencies; her highly developed sense of responsibility and the aggressive confidence with which she was taught by family models to express opinions). We have spent considerable time in candid discussion of the things each does which trigger our partner's reaction according to the syndrome.

2. Each of us has sought to get in touch with the personal feelings which seem to set the syndrome in motion. We have determined to learn how to share our feelings and how to listen to the other's feelings. It has been difficult to break old habits of laying out "headlines" (verbal pronouncements which rise out of pain, fear, anxiety, anger, or other deep feelings, but which mask the true story of the feelings behind them) and of reacting to expressed feelings with judgment, correction, or counterattack instead of empathy, understanding, and caring. Marriage Encounter (we experienced the Roman Catholic version) encouraged us to give high priority in our relationship to sharing and listening to one another's feelings, and helped us learn how to describe our real feelings to one another.

3. When either of us becomes aware that we have slipped into our "syndrome roles" again, we stop everything to point out what's happening. Sometimes this has been painful and led to hurt feelings and misunderstandings, but more often, it has been appreciated, and has enabled each of us to spot the "role play" in ourselves before it significantly disrupted communication.

4. We have shared our struggle with the church, confessing our sins to one another—in order to be healed (James 5:16). Others with the same problem have "come out of the woodwork." And we have found that we can help each other.

If the impression is coming through that this problem is totally solved and no longer ever interrupts the sheer bliss of our matrimonial tranquility, it is an erroneous impression. After all, we have only been aware of and working on this hang-up of ours for nine years! It had gotten a thirty-eight-year headstart (eighteen years in marriage), plus the effects of "the sin of the fathers [back] to the third and fourth generation!" (Exod. 20:5). If we are healed in this area in as few as ten more years it will still qualify as a miracle.

There have been changes in the pattern. Aware of the syndrome, its causes and preventions, aware of the things in us that have created and perpetuated it, we have discovered a greater variety of response-options at our disposal. We have greater freedom to choose an alternate course of action and reaction. This liberates us to concentrate on being lovers and friends.

> My wife is to be my wife. Not a substitute mother. I am to be near her for love, for the joy of being one, for sharing nuptial intimacies and for the sanctification possible through daily face-to-face interaction. Begone—my childish clamoring for something long dead—something for the man to leave behind among his "childish things" (1 Cor. 13:11).
> Lord, let it be.

Meeting One Another's Needs

When God created marriage and put man and woman together, it was not His idea that one man and one woman should be able to meet the totality of one another's needs. When He created marriage, He created the family as well. And, as we track His dealings with humankind through biblical history from Eden onward, we discover an intensifying interest in families. Not the mere nuclear family known and floundering today in Western culture, but *extended* families. Noah's family and Abraham's and Jacob's family of seventy-five souls, and so on. The extended family concept is emphasized by the geneologies of the Book of Numbers. Israel, the nation, is not so much a political entity as it is a clan, a great extended family.

Then Jesus announced that a new many-hundredfold family is being formed around Him (Mark 10:29–30). Acts describes this family from the moment of its birth, beginning in Acts 2. In Christ, the believer's primary clan, with all its gifts and resources available to meet family and personal needs, is the multi-faceted body of Christ—the living network of relationships bound together by the Holy Spirit in living relationship to the Father and His Son.

God intends for marriages to be close and strong, and for family members to be deeply committed to each other. Marriage is an important resource for meeting each other's needs and a stimulus for personal growth. But, by His design, the best marriage and the most healthy family is left with weaknesses and needs that can only be met in the context of a dynamic spiritual community which is rich in openness, freedom, and love.

My emotional immaturity, the struggle of Audrey and me to build a more healthy marriage—these are problems for the family of God to go through with us. Our needs are church needs. The resources from which we are to draw to confront these needs in our lives include not only those of Audrey and me and our kids, but the resources of the extended spiritual family.

God's design for the church is that, ultimately, no one be left unchanged or unhealed. His community, functioning as He plans, is a source of great power to effect genuine cures of human neuroses and psychoses, and the physical ailments which grow from them. The fact that the church, as many of us know it, is not such a healing community, should stimulate us to keep searching until we rediscover the spiritual principles that can turn that tragedy around.

The Right Sort of Independence

At the present time, my weaning is undergoing startling intensification. Not one or two but most of my attachments are being confronted. All my relationships and dependencies are being challenged: marriage, church, profession, friendships, commitments of various kinds, attachments to material things, locations, and traditions.

When I am fully weaned I expect *all* my substitute mothers will have been let go. I will have ceased clamoring for something to replace my mother's milk.

"Men of mature character," says James (1:4 Phillips), are characterized by "the right sort of independence." It's what the trauma of weaning is all about.

Even my relationship with God is in the throes of weaning. (Psalm 131 infers that it should be.) My Ultimate Parent cannot bend to my pleas that I be permitted to remain a babe-in-arms. Growth in Him leads to proper independence—not *from* Him, but *in* Him. He wants me to grow up until I no longer beg to "be fed" all the time. As maturity comes, I will see God as more than the supplier of my wants—a sort of "heavenly breast" dispensing what the spiritual baby needs. Instead, clamoring stilled, I will enjoy simply being with Him, resting on Him. Without always needing to suck.

What about my needs then? If I stop begging and reminding God of my wants, will He remember? Will they be supplied?

Psalm 131 exhorts simply, "O Israel, hope in the Lord from this time forth and forever." (v. 3 NASB).

A good mother does not need to be begged, only depended on in quiet confidence. With maturity comes the knowledge that our Heavenly Parent will feed us from His endless love that supplies all we truly need without fanfare. He finds His satisfaction (and assures ours) in a resting, hopeful delight in simply being close.

You mother me, Lord. Wean me from all my earthly mother-substitutes. Let me become a mature man of God, with the right sort of independence. Freed then to be a lover of God and a lover of my wife and a lover of the church.

> Brothers, stop thinking like children. In regard to evil be infants, but in your thinking be adults (1 Cor. 14:20).

CHAPTER 4

The Second Time Around

You know very well, my brothers (for I am speaking to those well acquainted with the subject), that the Law can only exercise authority over a man so long as he is alive. A married woman, for example, is bound by law to her husband so long as he is alive. But if he dies, then his legal claim over her disappears. This means that, if she should give herself to another man while her husband is alive, she incurs the stigma of adultery. But if, after her husband's death, she does exactly the same thing, no one could call her an adulteress, for the legal hold over her has been dissolved by her husband's death.

There is, I think, a fair analogy here. The death of Christ on the cross has made you "dead" to the claims of the Law, and you are free to give yourselves in marriage, so to speak, to another, the one who was raised from the dead, that we may be productive for God.

While we were "in the flesh" the Law stimulated our sinful passions and so worked in our nature that we became productive—for death! But now that we stand clear of the Law, the claims which existed are dissolved by our "death," and we are free to serve God not in the old obedience to the letter of the Law, but in a new way, in the Spirit (Rom. 7:1–6 Phillips).

It is not adultery to have a love affair with Jesus.[1]

> I have been "married" to "law" in the form of an antiquated, untrue-to-life picture of God. Picasso, painting through his uncorrected astigmatism, could not have left a more grotesque distortion of reality than the early shapers of my faith seem to have left in me of the character, methods, demands, and attitudes of the Bible's God.
>
> The God I have known best most of my life is a heavy-handed, unreasonably demanding, threatening, unaccepting "husband" to whom I seem to have been "married" as a child bride. I have always been in trouble with his way of measuring success or failure, because he has always demanded perfection. And perfection is one thing of which I have proven myself incapable.

My first husband's unrelenting perfectionism revolved around a lumpy mixture of (1) biblical commandments regarding performance and attitudes—i.e., perfect love as defined by First Corinthians 13:4–8, and perfect attitudinal patterns as defined in the Beatitudes; (2) added rules concerning "externals"—i.e., length of hair and skirts, wearing of gold and jewelry, abstinence from alcohol and tobacco, refrainment from worldly amusements and associations—all purportedly based on teachings of the Bible; plus (3) heavy doses of teaching on the judgment of God upon anyone who sins in any way—i.e., fails to keep the prescribed injunctions and mores.

Confusing, in a subliminal way, was the fact that the presenters of biblical instructions sometimes modeled the exact opposite of the attitudes which, for not possessing, we were being angrily castigated and threatened with judgment. The love-message was especially confusing. For this God, like the authority figures who taught us about Him, *said,* "I love you," in the poetry of King James English. But, in the next breath, He threatened utter rejection and horrible punishment if my life did not demonstrate the perfection He demanded. I soon learned that if someone says, "I love you," that means pain and rejection cannot be far behind! (It's a terrible distortion.

And it has stolen the joy from more personal relationships than I can count.)

The "added rules" consisted mostly of *deductions* from biblical statements rather than direct instructions of Scripture. Often, in reality, they were a neurotic response to some cultural evil, playing on the fears of simple people. Sometimes, I am convinced, they rose from a need to control others. Without exception, they demonstrated a colossal lack of understanding of the New Covenant, and about how spiritual reality becomes a part of a people. The extent of emphasis placed upon these "added rules" implicitly attached more importance to them than to the Gospel itself. And the emotional portrait of the God who was said to be behind them all became just that much more distorted and maddening.

Moral and spiritual perfection was not merely God's goal for us and His work in us, but unless it was achieved in our daily lives, there was really no hope of continuing in His good graces. "Grace" was something "won" by perfect obedience and perfect conformity. Allowances were made for ignorance and honest errors in judgment, and some forms of sin were cleverly redefined as mistakes, human weaknesses, "scars of the fall," and so on. But, for me, it was never enough to take away the persisting fear I lived with night and day that my willful and unwitting failures were placing me next in line for a free trip to hell!

The result in the lives of those who made up his "bride" was to reduce the important matter of separation from the world to the level of the ridiculous. They became "God's peculiar people" (1 Pet. 2:9 KJV)—even referring to themselves in those terms—but for the wrong reasons. Their predominant "strangeness" was not the beautiful uniqueness of a new relational community living a godlike lifestyle—i.e., returning good for evil, giving until they make themselves poor in behalf of needy others, offering one another support and freedom to come to full bloom as persons, loving one another enough to lay down their lives for the brethren, and loving God with joyful abandon (though I knew a few saints like that when I was growing up in the church).

But predominantly they seemed strange in their own eyes as

well as the world's because of the weird, antiquated dress of the women, the silly ways they wore their hair, the foolish means they employed to try to be "holy," the destructiveness of their mutual manipulations, and the strange outlets they found for the tensions created by their harsh, restrictive lifestyle (i.e., the wild "shouting spells" that often marked revival and camp meetings).

Quite unconscious of what they were doing, they made God seem capricious, inconsistant, and unreasonable. They sketched a dour figure who was more motivated by anger than love. In effect, they divided the Trinity: Jesus was gentle and loving and forgiving; God the Father was severe and quick to condemn; the Holy Spirit was easy to grieve, would depart at the slightest hint of sin, and worked in difficult-to-explain, narrowly restrictive ways.

> Because of my long marriage to this austere and joyless husband, my subconscious mind and vulnerable conscience still remind me that freedom, peace, and doing what brings me happiness, may actually be forms of spiritual adultery and of straying from pure love for my unsparing Master. But my enlightened conscious mind, freshly steeped in knowledge of the bright revelation of the *True* God in Jesus of Nazareth, now counters that these are responses of a psyche still wedded to a childhood religion of legalism, carried on under the name of Jesus Christ, but often not in touch with the real Jesus.

The real Jesus of Nazareth is the Word made flesh (John 1:14), God with us (Matt. 1:23), the true, intimate, accurate demonstration of God's reality. Jesus the God-man paints for us a portrait of God undistorted by the astigmatism of sin and legalism. The God He paints is a personal being intensely concerned about people and involved with them in their struggles as well as their victories. In Jesus, God is seen as the friend, not the enemy, of sinners. He is infinitely patient and loving with spiritual and physical cripples of all kinds, tender with the dull and erring, unashamed to be identified with the weak, powerfully equipped to heal and deliver and forgive, willing to go to extreme lengths to save lost people, loving so unconditionally that even as people rejected and defamed Him He forgave them and gave His life for them in the ultimate proof of God's love. In all of this, Jesus is the visible demonstration of the character and attitudes of the True God.

Now I am being told, in Romans 6, 7, and 8, that the granite-hearted, perfectionist husband of my youth is dead! He died with Jesus on the cross. He was buried. And he did not rise from the grave. He is forever dead.

My marriage to him is annulled.

I'm free!

Part of me still fears my dead husband's frown. Repeatedly, my conscience returns to the grave and hears the echo of his stern and condemning words. The old uncertainties inside me sit up in their coffins and demand attention. It is hard to remember that he is deceased. He still seems so alive in my sensibilities. Even when I am dreaming dreams of freedom and release, I wake to find his ghost still haunting me, still controlling many of my responses, motives, moods, perceptions, decisions, and feelings about myself . . . as though he were still living.

But he is dead. And any legal hold he had on me died along with him.

I do not, therefore, commit adultery when I run to the arms of my lover, the resurrected Jesus. Or when I welcome Him as my warm, tender, caring, personal friend. Or when I relax in His presence and let myself be what and who I am without pretension of any kind. Or when I celebrate His acceptance and take advantage of His forgiveness and count on His love . . . even though I am as imperfect as ever.

I am no adulteress when I forget—even reject outright—everything my old husband taught, or when I am deliberately careless about what he might think if he saw me doing this or that. I am not being unfaithful if I ignore the rules and traditions and formulas he laid down "for my good." I am not violating anything sacred if I stop responding to him in fear.

It is not adultery for me to take deep pleasure in simply knowing my lover and being with Him. Or to dare to think it brings Him enjoyment to be with me. When I share spiritual intercourse with my new husband, when all my secrets are known to Him, including every fault and sin, when I dare to be my naked, imperfect self with Him even though that means He embraces me with the extravagance of His perfect affection in the very presence of my uncovered ugliness and sin—it's all right.

Here is how it happened: At my old husband's demise, Jesus came down into the hellish depths where I was living in bondage, chose me for His own, made love to me in ways I had never known before (like my old husband never could), took me to Himself and rose up, taking me away with Him as His cherished bride.

And it is not promiscuity for me to enjoy this liberated love affair—even though I have been married before. It is lawful and right and holy and proper for me to love Jesus with my whole being and to become productive in bringing spiritual offspring to life by His Spirit. It is good for me to forsake the guilts and hardships of the former relationship with its outdated restrictions, for the airy new life of emancipation.

My old husband is dead. Gleefully, I may dance on his dusty grave. I am married now to the Everliving Jesus. And I'm free! Free to give myself, body and soul, in unashamed liberty and unrestrained totality to my new Lover. I'm free! Free to choose to live my life in response to the tender invitations of His love.

CHAPTER 5

Search for Giftedness (Part I)

Fan into flame the gift of God, which is in you (2 Tim. 1:6).

A tantalizing new hope is stirring inside—that it may be all right, even highly desirable, for me to be different.

The fact is, I *am* different.

It is not necessary for me to conform to the image of any other man. It is extremely important for me to know and accept who *I* am. What is *my* personality really like? Not the "public presence" I have learned to display—the dressed-up, carefully merchandised "me" that is little more than a composite of what the "significant others" in my life think I should be and do, and what society expects of a man in my position, of my age, living in my neighborhood, in my economic and educational strata.

As a compulsive people-watcher, I find delight in observing the passing parade of really varied people who live in the inner city. There is a rough beauty in the jumble of skin tones and lingual accents. Everyone's teeth are not all perfectly straight. Dress, by necessity and choice, does not conform to the latest catalog styles. Some of the inevitable pressures-to-conform which go with affluence are missing. There are harsh realities which call for the attention of politicians, social workers, and Christians, but when I look I see a freedom from expectation—the liberty to be strange, unique. (In the predominantly white, middle-to-upper class suburb where I live, there is often a numbing sense of sameness.)

Similarly, one of the joys of living in a small country town

59

(Miltonvale, Kansas, population 700) was the uniqueness the culture permitted. There was a freedom to be natural. There seemed to be a high level of acceptance offered to a broad variety of people. Value was given to the compulsive storyteller at the town's only cafe, whose yarns of past and present were always embroidered with a tangy variety of colloquialisms, each anecdote told in country-Kansas twang. "Ma"—the stubby, fiesty cook, who would loudly and good-naturedly argue with the customers from the kitchen where she plied her trade with great enjoyment and a complete absence of finesse—was expected to be the special character she was. There was acceptance for the village mongoloid, Georgie, as well as the banker (who seemed more aloof, tainted perhaps by too much association with Mammon, but nonetheless accepted in his uniqueness). These were really natural, special people—seemingly relishing each other's strangeness.

I am stranger than I have been permitted to be. The mold (sometimes it has felt like an iron maiden) into which I have been trying to fit is painfully uncomfortable. I am not what the expectations of my society and my enculturated conscience say I am.

Recently, for example, as I have purposely allowed the real me to float to the surface, I have been astonished to discover that despite the leadership role I have played, I am actually quite passive by nature. It explains much of the internal conflict which has dogged my tracks as a church leader. It feels strangely comfortable to acknowledge the truth that there is a very natural and normal part of me that is more at home in the role of responder and follower.

I'm not sure what this means. How does personal passivity mesh with the aggressiveness which is also undeniably part of my personality? Does this prophesy a new, unique shape of ministry for me, in which meaningful expression is found for both of these seemingly paradoxical attributes? Can I learn to accept myself both as the responsive, submissive follower *and* the assertive, aggressive leader?

I seem to hear God saying, "It is all right for you to be exactly who you are. I will accept and use what you really are (imperfect as that is) in a far more effective way than I have ever been able to use the unreal image you have been taught to project."

Giftedness[1]

The only way one can come into the body of Christ is to *live* his way into it. Jesus calls people to do more than believe. He expects them to respond, to live in His words. Only then are they considered genuine disciples (John 8:31, with context). The faith that saves is no mere mental or emotional assent to His being God's Son. It involves living in response to His Word as Lord. If a person responds to Christ, and begins living into all that He is, Jesus promises: That person will be free!

Such a living into or living out of this life effects a radical change:

> If anyone is in Christ, he is a new creation; the old has gone, the new has come! (2 Cor. 5:17).

The whole basis upon which we operate is different after we come into Jesus. Values and perspectives change.

We have a new internal motivational system. First, we are freed from the crushing burden of viewing life as a demand to be met. Instead, in Jesus, life is a gift to be feasted on (Rom. 6:23, 2 Cor. 9:15). Next, we are freed from the unconscious-but-constant attempt to make atonement for our inability to live up to the demands which press on us, by punishing ourselves or trying to justify ourselves for the way we are. Christ comes as *Savior*, not as accuser. The mood of life in Christ, therefore, becomes one of praise, gratitude, expectancy, freedom, wonder, newness. Each new day may be greeted with the expectant question, "What gift will be bestowed on me today?" rather than the anxious wondering what will be required today (Eph. 4:7–8).

All of this is the result of the gift of the Holy Spirit, who comes into our lives when we begin to follow Jesus Christ (Acts 2:28). Through this gift of the Spirit, a unique new self begins to emerge. Something special which was there, though imprisoned by the chains of sin and death, begins to break forth. The true, redeemed self begins to take shape. Spiritual rebirth adds the missing ingredient of God-relatedness, the spark of divine life, which brings to life and into reality and fullness the things which are essentially our true selves—those sensitive feelings, yearnings, tastes—the tenderer dimension of our humanness. New strengths begin to emerge, new consistencies, new capacities. A mysterious renewed being is fashioned—and at the heart of this "becoming" is the divine action: The Holy Spirit at work making us fully human. Jesus Christ the New Creator makes each of us something unlike any other creature fashioned by God—something wonderful, exciting, unique, and specifically needed in the total body of Christ.

This "charismatic" person is himself/herself a gift of the Holy Spirit to the church. Who and what we are, personally, in Christ, is the primary gift that each of us brings to the body, without which the body is immeasurably impoverished.

God has not created a single person whose being and uniqueness are not eternally needed. If the church is the full-orbed earthly reflection of the many-sided splendor of God (Eph. 3:10), every strange and special person-gift which may be discovered within the body becomes an indispensible and awesomely significant part of the great thing God is doing.

As fellow-members, then, our primary calling is to invite that priceless charism of personal uniqueness to come forth. "To love a person," writes Gordon Cosby, "means to help him recognize his uniqueness and to discover his gift."[2]

Cosby goes on to describe the characteristics of that kind of love, and of the community which can nurture such discovery and provide such emancipation to become what we are in Christ.

Freedom. Each person has a chance to discover his/her specialness, in a setting where heavy-handed "oughtness" is eliminated, and where our aim is that everyone be set free to "have the time of our lives doing what we want to do,"[3] the thing we are really equipped to do, the thing that brings us genuine joy.

Detachment. So that this miracle of the Spirit can take place, we will have to stop trying to control and manipulate the people in our lives—allowing the real person, the special thing the Spirit is creating in each life to blossom forth in freedom and in the exact image for which God's design calls.

Expectation. We are called, in the body, to take a new step of faith with each other. We are called to commit one another to God's care, God's love, and God's secret wisdom (Acts 14:23). We are to be "willing to trust God for whatever strange new work may emerge in the person we release."[4]

God has never intended all believers to look alike or do the same things. His plan is so marvelous that there is no way even to imagine the infinite variety of things He may be able to do in the life of a body of people who are really free to become whatever He brings forth. The church is a work of God. And no human mind has ever been created that can comprehend all of God, or can fathom all that He will do.

This profound truth is super-simplified in First Corinthians 12:4–6:

> There are different kinds of gifts, but the same Spirit.
> There are different kinds of service, but the same Lord.
> There are different kinds of working, but the same God works all of them in all men.

It's like saying, There are varieties of snowflakes . . . varieties of stars . . . varieties of faces. No two exactly alike. It is the way God does things.

Are there nine gifts (as listed in 1 Cor. 12:8–10)? Or twenty (the combined total of the four major gifts lists—1 Cor. 12:8–10, 28; Rom. 12:6–8; Eph. 4:11)? Whatever list one uses, whatever total at which one arrives, can be no more than a beginning. Each charism and each charismatic cluster becomes something different and special when it emerges from the uniqueness of each person-gift. Each of the Spirit's endowments comes to the body in an unlimited variety of talents and intelligences and personality traits, and flowing through an infinite variety of experiences and heredities which have shaped the person-gifts.

Trying to box all this into a neat theological package, trying to keep it all under some strong central control, or trying to manipulate and shape it so that our tiny human brains can "master" it all . . . is an exercise in futility.

If one of us were able to contain the whole of God, then I suppose that person would be capable of anticipating and describing all the many, many ways He will express Himself through people, and all the multiplied manifestations and gifts and expressions of personal distinctiveness that His new creation will give to the body. But that is not humanly possible. None of us is brilliant enough to comprehend all of God. So we must dare to release people to Him. And let Him create in and through them whatever strange new thing His infinity can conceive.

Giftedness and What I Want To Do

One statement by Gordon Cosby has richocheted around in my head ever since I first read it:

> I think all of us had best find out what we really want to do and start doing it, with whatever that involves. If you have to give up your responsibility, give it up; if the church goes to pieces, so be it. But we've got to find what we want to do, *really*, because nothing else is going to help anybody.[5]

Just this week I read a similar statement by Dr. Smiley Blanton, the psychologist, in a book he co-authored with Norman Vincent Peale:

> To be successful one must be willing first of all to learn what he wishes to do. Then, after having gained the consent of his unconscious mind as he has of his conscious mind, he can bend his unobstructed energy to it. Every man has a right to be happy in his own way so long as it is not socially destructive. Too often we are deflected by the will and attitude of other people about what constitutes success . . . We cannot be content if a ruthless taskmaster either inside us or outside us deflects us from what is the most satisfactory fulfilment of our needs.[6]

"Yes! Yes!" my eager spirit shouts with serendipitous joy. But . . .

The first flush of hope upon consideration of such an idea quickly turns to a flame of frustration—at times a towering inferno of rage—when I return to my work in the church. For there, dreams of freedom and fulfilment are immediately confronted with certain high, barbed-wire-crowned realities.

First, there is little encouragement in the institutional structure for a man to spread wings and fly in a style of life and work truly consistent with personal giftedness. Within tightly restrictive boundaries some freedom is allowed, but almost never at the sacrifice of any institutional or cultural expectations. What, for instance, is the church to do with a minister who feels called to preach and shepherd, but feels neither called nor gifted for organizational administration? He is expected "by virtue of office" to be an administrator, whether or not he is gifted for it. He is expected to leave the things he wants to do for the things that "must be done."

Another reality which frustrates the quest for true fulfilment is my inner emotional and evaluative machinery which automatically denies permission for me to consider what I might *want* to do with my life. A chief hibition dourly declares from within, "A man who leaves the ministry for another vocation is being disobedient to God and a disgrace to the church." But is it conceivable that a man, in his maturity, might discover spiritual capabilities and limitations which indicate greater usefulness in an occupation different from the one he chose in his immaturity? Such thoughts are quickly countered by conscience's restatement of the unwritten law: "No place could possibly be more fulfilling or useful than the professional ministry."

Still another reality can turn hope into confusion or anger: There are aspects of this work—the professional pastoral ministry as conceived in our culture—for which I have personal loathing. There are things I am expected to do well for which I feel abysmally unequipped, charismatically and emotionally. And when I, in response to the expectations of others, engage in these areas of "ministry," I sometimes force myself into practices which violate personal honesty and spiritual priorities. I feel cheated and used—prostituted. I feel coerced by the system to cheat the people to whom I am "ministering," who, instead of getting a gift are being given a shoddy substitute for reality.

For example, every good pastor is expected to engage in an effective ministry of counseling. But I have never felt comfortable in the role of "counselor." I have felt woefully inadequate, like the blind man groping in unfamiliar territory, almost certain to lead himself and those following him into the proverbial ditch. A small amount of specific training and much reading have not taken away the feeling of being unprepared and unequipped for the counseling ministry.

But I have tried anyway. My datebook has been crowded with "counseling appointments." I have played counselor. I have sat behind a desk taking notes, employing techniques picked up at the latest seminar. I have manipulated people's emotions, asking probing personal questions ... and felt lost and phony. For me, the role is bigger-than-life. In it I inevitably find myself trying to be what I am not.

I have dreaded counseling appointments and am nearly always delighted to be "stood up" by a counselee. I hate myself in the role I feel forced to play, because of the denial of reality inherent in the situation. The tensions caused by the numbers of people who look to me for guidance which I feel unequipped to give are devastating in my personal life. But fear of falling short of the expectations that go with the office drives me to continue.

Amazingly, some people have said they were helped in those "counseling sessions." And I have truly wanted that—to help people. But, for me, "counseling"—as a "professional"—is not the way. It is clear that many people *need* counsel. But am I (the pastor) the only one in the body of Christ equipped to give it? And is the "counselor-counselee" setting the only acceptable or effective place for it?

Instead ... let's get together as friends at my house or yours. Let's drink a cup of coffee together—or go for a walk—and talk over whatever you want to talk over. I'll accept you and I'll listen and I'll care. I'll share whatever insights and answers I have discovered. I'll share the way I'm struggling with a similar problem. We'll search the Scriptures together for insights. We'll pray for one another and pledge support to one another. But not as "counselor" and "patient." Let's be friends and brethren, fellow-strugglers, who need each other. But don't call me for a "counseling appointment." (I'll freeze up and put on my phony face.) And, please, allow me the freedom to tell you when my circuits are overloaded, and when I think someone else can help you as well as or better than I.

I can give you the gift of friendship and listening, and share myself with you at depth. Don't force me to give you the cheap substitute of merely playing out some unrelated, pre-written script.

I do not mean to minimize in the least the Holy Spirit's sovereign ability to work through even ill-equipped, emotionally-crippled people, or people out-of-place. The Scriptures record many incidents in which the situation demanded grace beyond what the most unlikely people seemed to possess. But the Spirit ministered through them in powerful, life-changing ways. God does these things. Furthermore, even the best-prepared and most effectively wrought ministry has inherent weaknesses which remind mere humans of how dependent on Him they always are.

> It seems to me that my working years have known too much dissatisfaction and frustration. A high level of compulsion has motivated much of my work. There is a growing feeling that for too much of my life as a Christian I have been doing what was expected of me and leaving undone what genuinely fulfils and delights me.
>
> There are facets of "the ministry" I have actually enjoyed. Parts of the work I feel good about. I'm even "good at" some of it. But there are also significant parts I have hated. Though, of course, a "man of God" would never express such feelings for "the high calling"—at least not openly—scarcely even to himself. So I have buried such feelings, along with "other sinful thoughts and passions," below the level of consciousness, where undealt with, they continue to eat at my life from the inside. Not until recently have I dared to face my true attitudes on the conscious level.
>
> Psychologists say that intense feelings which are denied sometimes find expression in a subconscious "will to fail." Smiley Blanton, for example, tells of a man who was emotionally manipulated to forsake the teaching career he'd dreamed of and for which he had spent years preparing, to

go into business with his father. Inwardly, he hated the business and his father for deflecting him from what he really wanted to do. But, for a long while, he denied these feelings and succeeded in business. Then his father died. While still pursuing the business in his father's name, he began to make fiscal decisions which seemed calculated to bring the business down. A proven astute business man, he was unconscious of the dynamite going off inside. Eventually the business failed altogether, amid a scandal which brought litigations which finally cost him all he had earned through the secretly hated enterprise.

I am not a psychologist, and so I am not certain of the accuracy of my self-diagnosis, but I have been aware of some things surfacing in my life which make me wonder if something has been going on in me that is somehow akin to the experience of the man in Blanton's story. Could the frustration I feel with "my life's work" be so deep that even while I consciously seek to "fulfil my calling," my subconscious mind—more in tune with the real emotional climate inside me—has been programming me to fail so that I can be free to escape the bondage of an unwanted "call"?

The human heart is capable of this kind of massive self-deception! (See Jer. 17:9.)

I have been vaguely conscious of such secret inner sabatoge at times when my "nerves" have given 'way (or I have given 'way to my nerves), when emotions have run rampant, temporarily rendering me unable to function in ministry. At two such times I cancelled important speaking trips at the last moment and escaped to some hideaway to put myself back together again. At another time, I resigned one church to flee to another. At other times, only my family suffered directly with my collapse.

Today, I was reading John 5:1–15, the story of the impotent man at the Pool of Bethesda. He had been lying there an invalid for thirty-eight years waiting to be healed, blaming others for not helping him into the healing waters. (I felt a strange identification with this man who had remained crippled well into mid-life.)

Jesus asked, "Do you want to be healed?"

I paused in my reading. I seemed to hear Him asking the same question of me: "Do you *want* to be healed?"

I was shocked at the response I heard coming from inside. "I don't know," I said. "If it means I will never get free from the responsibilities of church leadership, I do not know if I want to be healed!"

At that moment I remembered that there had been other times, when in the midst of some trauma, the thought had crossed my mind that if I could simply go "stark, raving mad," no one would any longer expect the things they now expect of me, which cause such fear, frustration, and discontent.

And there was one time, when, in a desperate inner storm of guilt and inadequacy, feeling as though the overwhelming weight of responsibility for the church would crush me, and with no visible hope for escape from the pressure, I actually, for a short time, considered finding someone with whom to have an adulterous affair. I had no one in particular in mind. There was no one I wanted other than my wife. But, for a brief, insane moment, I fancied that if I were to commit such a sin, my clerical career would be over. I would, at last, be "free."

Soundness of mind prevailed. I realized the madness of it, how satanic the thought was and how terribly destructive it would be for my marriage and my family, as well as the church. So never did it develop into more than desperate thought. But the fact that I could consider such a thing—even briefly—was, to me, evidence of deep spiritual sickness at the point of my "life's work."

I can no longer deny the intense basic yearning to escape the distasteful aspects of "the ministry," which rob me of joy and lead to deep depression. As bad as they might seem, my real attitudes must be brought into the light, faced and dealt with, by faith. For the discomfort of exposure cannot compare with the potential disaster which is possible when intense emotions are habitually denied.

The intensity with which I felt these frustrations drove me to some in-depth heart-searching to discover my true motivations and, if possible, the things I would rather be doing with my life. If the Bible's teaching on giftedness has anything to do with fulfilment and joy in the work one is pursuing in the church, then something is decidedly wrong with the match-up between me and my work.

When the early decisions were being made, I was seeking to please God in my choice of vocation. Considering the circumstances, it may have been the only response He could have expected from me at the time. I have been grossly unhappy in it and have suffered immense pain over parts of it simply because my personal gifts and heart's desires did not really fit the demands of pastoral ministry (as the institution and the culture have shaped those demands). What I now know about myself tells me I could be happier and more effective doing something else in the church. God, in His sovereign grace, has used me where I did not belong. But now He is setting me at liberty to discover a richer ministry in which I can be who I am and do what I am best suited to do.

However, His process of giving me the freedom He always wanted me to have will necessarily involve changes in my unconscious mechanisms of response.

Bondage to tradition and to others' expectations is set so deeply in me, I cannot respond to His new light without an inner miracle of emancipation.

The Desires of Your Heart

How can it be true that discovering what one wants to do is a key to discovering what God wants done and what needs to be done? To me it sounds too good to be true. Does it really square with reality?

Paul, in his conflict-ridden testimony of Romans 7 seems to be describing how fundamentally untrustworthy the heart of man—even of a Christian—is. But there is a glowing key half-buried in this pile of battle junk.

> ... I am unspiritual, sold as a slave to sin. I do not understand what I do. For what I want to do I do not do, but what I hate I do ... I know that nothing good lives in me, that is, in my sinful nature. For I have the desire to do what is good, but I cannot carry it out. For what I

do is not the good I want to do; no, the evil I do not want to do—this I keep on doing. Now if I do what I do not want to do, it is no longer I who do it, but it is sin living in me that does it.

So I find this law at work: When I want to do good, evil is right there with me. For in my inner being I delight in God's law (Rom. 7:14–15, 18–22).

Is there escape from this wretched pattern of failure?

Thanks be to God—through Jesus Christ our Lord! (Rom. 7:25).

I am hearing something in Paul's testimony I have never heard before—an exciting serendipity. In the very presence of the ugly litter of warfare and stinging defeat lies a subtle key to renewal of the believer's inner response pattern:

What *I want* to do . . . what *I hate* . . . (v. 15)
What *I do not want* to do . . . (v. 16)
I have the desire to do what is good . . . (v. 18)
The good I want to do . . . the evil I do not want to do . . . (v. 19)
What *I do not want* to do . . . (v. 20)
I want to do good . . . (v. 21)
In my inner being I delight in God's law . . . (v. 22)
I myself in my mind am a slave to God's law . . . (v. 25)

An amazing revelation! Since becoming a follower of Jesus Christ there is a part of me that wants what God wants. Through the Spirit's operation a new creation totally tuned to God and in full accord with His will is rising from the rubble of the old life. The new creation is marked by a whole new set of "want-to's" which are in perfect harmony with God's plan.

Warfare persists in that the old thought patterns and the old devil-dominated, sin-shaped desires also tug at me, trying to drag me away from the God-shaped longings of the new humanity. Paul calls these old sin-bent wants "lusts" (Rom. 7:8 NASB margin). They consist of carnal hungers; selfish motivations; sensual fancies; once-legitimate human desires gone rebellious; worldly, God-ignoring appetites born and shaped in me by the pre-Christian inputs and experiences of my life. Generations of fallen human heritage, years of sin-affected parental modeling, personal observation of cultural "norms," instruction in worldly wisdom, and personal choices have taught me to want my God-less wants. And they were not automatically turned off when I met Jesus.

Since meeting Him, however, a new life in Him, a new mind set on the Spirit, is breaking up the ancient internalized laws for living with God. Now I live in the glow of the promise of new victories over the old humanity, and of my ultimate unveiling before the whole created universe as a completed, totally renewed, marvelously changed child of God, like Jesus in every way (Rom. 8:1–30).

Because there is a part of every born-again believer that wants what God wants, an extremely important aspect of spiritual growth involves getting in touch with the new self and its Spirit-wakened desires.

Through the years, I have read several seemingly unbelievable biblical statements which bear on this matter. I have felt I was touching one of the keys to abundant living, but have been afraid to grasp and use it. How dare a sinner like me trust his deep desires and feelings? Have I not been taught to say No to them? And for good reason: Look at all the "nuts" running around claiming that the silly or wrong or weird things they are doing are things God told them to do! "The heart [of man] is more deceitful than all else and is desperately sick; Who can understand it?" cried Jeremiah (17:9 NASB). How true! I have been deceived by my own false motives and self-centered desires, repeatedly. And I have observed this same tendency toward self-deception in almost everyone I know.

But then . . . what is this?

> *David:* O Lord . . . Thou hast given me my heart's desire,
> And Thou hast not withheld the request of my lips
> (Ps. 21:2 paraphrased).
> May He grant you your heart's desire,
> And fulfil all your counsel [margin: purpose] (Ps. 20:4 NASB).
> Delight yourself in the LORD;
> And He will give you the desires of your heart
> (Ps. 37:4 NASB).
> He will fulfil the desire of those who fear Him
> (Ps. 145:19 NASB).

Jesus: If you remain in me and my words remain in you, ask whatever you wish, and it will be given you (John 15:7).

Paul: Continue to work out your salvation with fear and trembling, for it is God who works in you to will [to create desire and positive volition] and to act according to his purpose (Phil. 2:12-13, brackets added).

Oswald Chambers comments on this Pauline statement:

> When the Holy Spirit comes in, He energizes a man's will, He works in him to will to want to do the will of God. The deliverance is a very profound and practical one, God alters my 'want to,' i.e., the ruling disposition —by introducing His own will into me.[7]

Getting in Touch With the New Creation

It is absolutely essential, then, that we "get in touch with ourselves." And this "getting in touch" must include knowledge and confession of our inner sinful patterns and propensities as well as the holy "want to's" stirring in us from God.

Most Christians seem afraid to look at themselves. Because of fear and hurt and sin, they have buried their deepest feelings and desires. (It is one of the ways the world around us has pressed us into its mold—our society is like this.) Instead of becoming fully human (which is what Christ has set us free to be) many are still afraid to feel their own true feelings. They are even more afraid to *show* them. As though some sinister danger, some unbearable pain, some dark disappointment lies in ambush ready to leap out and destroy if such self-revelation were to be permitted. The first sad result of this great cover-up is that the cleansing (Greek: purification and integration) from all sin (1 John 1:7, 9) is hindered by self-chosen darkness. And, further, along with our feelings, we have buried our dreams and hopes and uniqueness beneath the wet blanket of imposed responsibility and smothering conformity.

If what Cosby and Blanton and David and Jesus and Paul and I have been saying is true, then these fears of self-disclosure still clung to and these imposed coverings still unflung, are actually hindering the unveiling of the unique and wonderful new work the Holy Spirit is creating in us.

This truth calls for a new depth of openness and honesty in our lifestyles and in all our relationships. "Paradoxically," writes Cecil Osborne, "We come to know ourselves in *the act of self-disclosure* . . . In disclosing ourselves to 'significant others' we discover our true identity."[8]

We shall have to help each other in this. In the church and in the family, a new level of commitment to each other is needed.

> No matter how much we love a person, accept him, give him support, have warmth and affection for him, no matter how much we help him in so many ways, unless we can actually call *him* forth, so that he is *himself*, exercising the uniqueness God gave him, then the love is incomplete; he is not free, he is less than fully human (Gordon Cosby).[9]

It has got to begin to matter to us about each other. We must start to see and act on the vision that if our brother, sister, spouse, or child is not free to be himself/herself, it invariably inhibits our own spiritual maturity and richness and power. When one person is too bound to share his uniqueness, the body is crippled and divided (1 Cor. 12:14–26).

CHAPTER 6

Search for Giftedness (Part II)

We have different gifts, according to the grace given us. If a man's gift is prophesying, let him use it in proportion to his faith (Rom. 12:6).

A New Dream for Ministry

Early in our church's corporate process of renewal and restructuring, a new ideal of ministry began to form in my thinking. The questions we were asking about the church stimulated questions about ministry—what it is and how it functions in the biblical church. As others began to discover freedom and authority to move into their priesthood and began to grasp how they were equipped and called to serve one another's needs, I began to thirst for liberation from traditional pastoral role-playing. Discomfort with certain of the role's demands intensified. I began to yearn for a niche in God's plan for the church into which I might fit as if I was made for it and it for me.

I found myself dreaming of a natural style of pastoring in which I could be totally free to be myself. A work in which effective ministry would take place in the context of real friendships between people who are not "clergy" and "laity" but brothers (Matt. 23:8-12). I longed to relax and be human. I wanted to be able to say No to those who ask me to serve beyond the grace and gifts I have been given (Rom. 12:3, 6). I ached to feel comfortable acknowledging my limitations.

I could see us touching one another in spiritual ministry,

with dirty hands, while we worked together at the common projects of our lives. I could visualize a mutual style of spiritual care in which, while I served the needs of others, they, knowing about my needs, served mine.

Teaching and preaching would grow out of our day-to-day experience with God and each other, and would often be simply the sharing of that experience along with the biblical principles it illustrates or which apply to it. Presentation of the teaching would be extremely informal, permitting interaction of the other believer-priests with the one designated as teacher. I fancied the freedom to teach only when I have something alive and pressing to say, rather than being forced to preach by an arbitrary schedule. (I have never been able to escape the admonition of a Methodist bishop who challenged his preachers not to preach until they had "something to say which must be said or the stones will cry out!")

There was no wish to be less spiritual or sanctified or Christian. I merely wanted it all to be real—to flow from the realities of my relationship with God and His people.

Our church's restructuring stimulated such fantasies and made possible the relational groundwork necessary to move toward their realization. Part of our renaissance was in the structure of church leadership. A team of elders replaced the pastor-and-church-board type of organization. From the time of their selection it was envisioned that the elders would assume, not merely the policy-making function, but eventually would serve the church together as its shepherds. They were called "The Pastoral Team" to emphasize this goal.

Team leadership meant that my dominant place as leader would gradually give place to leadership by this cadre of several men. My ministry would merge into that of the team, in which each elder would seek to develop a pastoral ministry in keeping with his gifts and the effects of his service in the lives of people. This also meant that I could ease out of the areas of work for which I felt unequipped—allowing others with the gifting to serve there. My energies and time could be concentrated in the direction of my personal giftedness.

It was not as easy as that. The culture, the denomination, the parishioners' expectations, and my own overblown sense of responsibility still made demands without regard to giftedness or the Holy Spirit's design.

But I did find courage, tentatively at first, to dare to say No sometimes, giving the others on the team a chance to say Yes. They did not match every No of mine with a Yes of theirs, and this left some things undone—but they applauded me, and kept urging me to do what I felt I ought to do regardless of tradition or popular expectation. They stood by me when others could not understand this process. And they gradually assumed more and more of the pastoral load. Their support gave me gradually increasing courage to respond to the desires of my heart.

One of the things the team did, while in its developmental stage, was to attend a Dynamic Church Seminar in California led by Larry Richards and David Mains. A very significant moment in my search for giftedness came at that meeting. One of David Mains' lecture-subjects concerned the discovery of Spiritual Gifts. As part of his presentation he gave each participant a sheet of paper with four sets of lines on it, for making four lists. On the first set of lines we were told to "list the abilities or potential gifts you have."

Dutifully, I complied, listing . . .
1. Teaching
2. Pastoral ministry
3. Music/singing
4. Administration
5. Counseling
6. Prophecy: sharing the vision God has given me for the renewal of the church
7. Writing
8. Evangelism

The second list called for "Areas of need in the church I perceive." I listed several.

The third set of lines became most significant. Mains instructed us to look again at the list of "potential gifts" and, this time, to list them in the order of their importance to us, personally.

"Start the list with *the one gift you cannot give up*."

As I worked with the gift list from this perspective, I discovered to my amazement that I could give up all of them . . . except one. The one thing I felt I must do, the one "gift" I could not live without because it was so integrally a part of me, was the thing I called "prophecy," which I had earlier defined as "sharing the vision God has given me for the renewal of the church."

The fourth list was to note the "areas of need" (from list 2) which our gifts indicated we might be able to serve.

The seminar moved to its conclusion. We all went back to our work in the church.

I did not think about gifts until a week later, when the discovery I'd made began to "nag" me. "The one gift I cannot give up is prophecy. Yet that is precisely the point of frustration and pain, because that gift seems so often to be submerged beneath a mountain of pastoral responsibilities for which I wonder if I am gifted at all."

With that conflict in mind, I sat down to write my feelings.

> I believe my most important gift (the one I cannot give up) is prophecy (i.e., sharing the vision God has given me for the renewal of the church). Given the person I am—my talents, skills and limitations, and my present placement in the body—the gift of prophecy, as I understand it, could best be developed and used in the following areas of ministry:
>
> 1. *Writing.* I believe God has given me a writing ministry, but, for the most part, I am kept so busy doing other things in "the ministry" that I seldom, if ever, do any writing.
>
> 2. *Teaching.* The kind which sets forth broad biblical principles and perspectives. I should not do more than half the teaching in our local church. The church needs more than my "prophetic" style. There is a need for down-to-earth teaching which touches the practical aspects of living: problem-solving, decision-making, marriage and family issues, the how-to's of a hundred different parts of life. Whenever I try to deal with these things, my teaching invariably focuses on broad concepts, and is weak in practical application. I am forced to depend on the interaction of the body to apply the truth to everyday life. I do not appear to be strongly gifted in that area.

3. *Radio or television ministry.* Broadcasting aimed at the church at large and its need for renewal.

4. *Sharing my vision with the elders of our local church.* In the church at Antioch, teachers and prophets ministered side by side in the leadership group (Acts 13:1).

5. *Teaching the biblical concepts of church life outside our local church.* My ministry is rooted here. But I have a growing sense of oneness with and concern for the body of Christ wherever it is, both in and outside of the established churches. I wish to be available to assist in the renewal process wherever my gifts can be of help.

I am frustrated in the following ministry areas, leading me to wonder if they are not outside my spiritual giftedness:
1. Church administration
2. Counseling (as it is usually perceived)
3. Practical teaching
4. Pastor of the church
5. Evangelist

Upon further reflection, I think I may be spiritually gifted in one or two of these areas. My frustration in these cases may stem, not from being unequipped, but from hearing God saying things to me, to which I am not free to respond, because I am "covered up" with doing alone what others in the body are also equipped to do. Were each member emancipated to pursue his/her priestly office, I too could be emancipated to follow what I hear Him saying to me.

Possible Practical Suggestions for the church rising from these conclusions:

1. *Church administration.* Elders (other than myself) assume leadership of elders' and deacons' meetings.

2. *Counseling.* (a) Provide more training in counseling for members of the body. (b) Add to the church staff a trained Christian counselor.

3. *Pastoring and teaching.* (a) Elders move more forthrightly to assume the full pastoral burden of the church. (b) Pursue discovery and development of teachers from the local congregation, and give them a greater role in the

teaching ministry. (c) If needed, add to the church staff a gifted pastor-teacher, whose ministry can fill some of the gaps in our present didactic and shepherding work. (Specific names were attached.)

    4. General. I am willing to go off salary if necessary to make these changes possible.

The response of the elders and others with whom I shared these insights and suggestions was positive. All encouraged me to pursue the kind of ministry which my personal giftedness seemed to blueprint. Some of the "Possible Practical Suggestions" blossomed and bore fruit: 1) A five-minute broadcast on a local religious radio station, which daily for one year aired a "prophetic" message calling for renewal of the church; 2) Increased frequency of the use of other gifted body members to teach and preach and lead the meetings; 3) The Ministry Team (elders) have assumed full administrative and pastoral leadership of the church; 4) Several men and women are developing significant counseling ministries, with some involving themselves in specific training for their growing ministries; 5) Significant curtailment of my time-commitment to the local church, making time available to pursue my writing; and 6) By my own choice and for reasons I'll explain later in this chapter, I became an unsalaried member of the pastoral team.

All these things have been valuable in the search for my true giftedness, and for the freedom that goes with knowing who one is and where one fits.

"What Am I Going To Be When I Grow Up?"

In the fall of 1977, I was thrust by the Holy Spirit into still another phase of my personal gift discovery (and self-discovery) process. In Chapter 2 (p. 29) I told how, while listening to a message with some friends, God's Spirit unmasked before the eyes of my soul the depth of my spiritual poverty. I had to confess before the others how full obedience was beyond my present spiritual reach. Because inside me, newly exposed, were firmly-constructed, stubbornly resistant emotional strongholds, over which I seemed to have little or no control, which fought Christ's way of thinking and doing as though to surrender would mean destruction of me as a person. Fear was dominating a great many of my spiritual responses. Part of me wanted to respond, but full obedience was out of the question until these inner response systems could be brought into the light, healed, and made to bow to the authority of Jesus.

I had said the words of commitment and surrender many times. I had thought that I was flying the white flag over all of my life. To be sure, each prior yielding had left its positive mark on my spiritual structure. But at this particular moment I saw how shallow my relinquishment really had been. I saw, too, that I did not really know who I am.

I cannot surrender to God any part of myself which I do not understand or own.

The months that followed have been a time of search and discovery. A personality test, the commitment of others to go with me through whatever the search involved, the support of my wife, the freedom offered me by my local church and its leaders, and the faithfulness of the Holy Spirit to break in with needed insights at key points, have all been part of the process.

It has been a time for basic questions which, it seemed to me, should have been answered in adolescence—Who am I? What am I really like? Why am I like I am? What are my true feelings? What are my real motives for doing what I am doing? What do I want to do with my life? Why am I a Christian? A minister? A husband? *What do I want to be when I grow up?* What about my relationship with God, the church, my wife, and other people, is real and what is merely a "put on" to keep myself and other people from finding out the truth about me? What is love? Do I know anything at all about how to love? Do I love anyone but myself? Do I even love myself?

It has been an uprooting, insecure, not-knowing-where-to-go-next kind of experience. My cage has been rattled. And all my relationships have been shaken up—including my relationship with God.

One very "dangerous" question emerged from inside—it had been there for a very long time, though never expressed openly: Would God still love me if I were not "in the ministry"? Can I be a Christian and not be a "minister"?

It brewed and boiled beneath the surface for a while. Then one evening at a group meeting, it erupted in open confession. It was as though the lid had blown off a tank of fermenting bitterness. In tears, I confessed before this small group of members of my church the feeling of being trapped in the ministry, of personal inadequacy, of ministerial prostitution of my gifts and personality, of hatred for parts of the task for which I felt unequipped and mis-assigned, of frustration over my own limitations and inability to change, and of fear that if I tried to do anything else with my life God would surely be displeased and withdraw His love from me, and people too would reject me.

The group, mostly young adults, were amazingly sensitive. They had no easy answers, no advice to offer. Only the assurance that they loved me, that they really felt what I was feeling. They encouraged me to act on the true inner feelings I had expressed. They would support me and love me whatever course I decided to take, even if it meant leaving the ministry altogether.

Out in the open now, this issue—so basic to the direction of my life and that of the church—could no longer be ignored. Soon the whole church was aware of my uncertainty and concern. Each member of the body, to the degree of his understanding, became involved with me in my struggle. My being "in the ministry" must be based on solid spiritual reality, not on the expectations of my peers or what might please my mother or my need to be "someone significant." Had God spoken to me? Or had He and I been merely "making the best" of a second-best situation? Did my real feelings, my true heart's desires, and my actual gifting from the Holy Spirit portend a different life's direction for me?

"These are teen-age questions and should have been answered long ago—before I spent twenty-five years in 'full time Christian service'!" I berated myself.

"Many people struggle with such questions in mid-life," was the answer from a trusted friend and psychologist.

The tension and insecurity this search brought into my

home was agonizing for my family. Audrey struggled painfully with it, but knew I was dealing with issues which must be dealt with. In the face of her own insecurity concerning the changes taking place, and not knowing what the costs were going to be, she renewed her commitment to me, verbalizing her determination to stick with me through whatever I had to do to find emotional health and spiritual reality. If it meant leaving the ministry or the church, she would go along. If it meant a whole new way of life, she would be with me. Even if it cost the break-up of our marriage for me to find out who I am and what I want to do, she would trust God with it and live with it.

Without her support and that of the church, this whole process could have led to disaster. But God is faithful and He is Reality. Any honest search for Reality ultimately leads to Him. He provided what I needed. And I have needed Audrey and the church at this time more than ever before in my life.

In late spring, with the support of the elders and the prayers of the church, I began a "sabbatical" of undetermined duration. It was to be a time free from all church responsibilities. An opportunity to sort out my newly awakened feelings, to give attention to my personal relationship with God, and to evaluate "the ministry" and my future.

The Day My "Sabbatical" Began

Today I begin what I hope is a new phase of my life. It is the start of a "leave" from pastoral duties. Others are calling it "sabbatical," "furlough," "vacation," "time off," "escape" —whatever comforts them.

I see it differently. It is a chance for me to leave the old patterns of professional life behind and enter, *permanently,* a whole new thing.

I have dreams and hopes for this time . . .

First, I don't see it as a "time." Today I begin a whole new approach to life. I do not ever expect to "come back" to the professional ministry—not even as I have known it in its "renewal" sense. I wish to be free to be whatever God wants me to be in the church.

There is a sense in which I am running away. I am escaping from responsibilities (and *the* responsibility) I no longer wish to carry. What a millstone around my neck "pastoral responsibility" has been! At times I'd have been willing to fight God to get free from it. And yet, I feel selfish and defeated about the decision to leave it. But I don't know if I should feel that way.

On the positive side, I believe I am running away from ineffectiveness and from the *world's* expectations, from ungiftedness, from dead, killing tradition, and from insensitivity to the voice of God. (I think my sensitivity to God's voice has been dulled by the voices of preconceived ideas about church and ministry, by socially-formed mindsets that have no relation to nor concern for what God is saying, and by prior commitments made before I understood either the nature of the church or the nature of ministry.) I am running away from trying to be something/someone I was never created to be.

I expect some things from this "leave." Christ promised newness of life—I have a vision of the emergence of a new man . . .

The new man is free.
> Free to be who he is.
> Free to take responsibility for himself and allow others to take responsibility for themselves.
> Free to do what he deeply desires to do.
> Free to be effective.
> Free to make his own choices, to speak his own mind.
> Free to relate to God and others on his own terms and out of his own uniqueness.
> Free to discover what his true gifts are.
> Free to let the Holy Spirit shape a unique ministry with unique effects, suited to and flowing from the positive strangeness of who he is and what he really has to work with.

The new man is free from the old destructive personality patterns: aggression, hostility, stored-up anger, unresolved hatred, fear of criticism, fear of not being listened to, hatred of self, depression, dependency (inordinant dependence on others for approval, identity, worth, direction), avoidance of responsibility, poor self-concept.

> I envision a man who knows and is sufficiently comfortable with himself to be able to respond to God and his own inner desires without harrassment from doubts and fear of what others are going to think.
>> A man who can take criticism without defensiveness, anger, and depression.
>> A man who doesn't have to succeed in the eyes of the world to feel good about himself.
>> A man who can accept himself as he is . . .
>> Fat or thin
>> Smart or dumb
>> Weak or strong
>> Inadequate or able
>> Succeeding or failing.
>
> An impossible dream? It's mine. I am a fool, but not foolish enough to think all this can happen in the next few months or a year. But I expect release from the "unreasonable" demands of "the ministry" to allow time to address these issues and to make visible progress.

When the leave began, it was with full financial support. But the umbilical cord of support seemed to keep me in bondage to the old expectations. So July 1, in order to be "free from all men" (Paul cites this as his reason for refusing support in Corinth, 1 Cor. 9:18–19), I asked that my salary be discontinued. I wished to be free from the sense of obligation which goes with salary, in order to see if I could hear more clearly what God might be saying to me about the shape of His plan for me.

There was a sense of adventure in all of this. When my "sabbatical" began, I had not decided whether to secure regular employment. I checked into several job possibilities. But, instead, we decided to follow a dream. For some time I had fantasized a full-time career as a writer. Writing was one gift I felt confident was mine. There was no assurance of adequate income or security on such a course. (Not many Christian writers make enough to live on from writing alone.) But, at age forty-seven, Audrey and I decided if I was ever going to "try my wings" in such a venture, it had better be sooner than later. So, with "now or never" echoing through my searching brain, and with a sense of peace with God that it was the right thing to do, we decided to take the risks involved. (It must be added, however, that the local church's new style of life gave us assurance that we would be taken care of by our spiritual family, should our needs require material or financial help.)

My "sabbatical" gave the elders new freedom to assume full pastorship of the church. When I returned, I was not to jump back into the old role. I was to stay loose. I was to ease my way into a ministry shaped according to my true gifts and heart's desires. I would return as a member of the Pastoral Team if I wished, but there were to be no strings attached. What the church and the leaders wanted was a "Bob Girard-shaped" ministry, in which there would be no more prostitution, and in which there would be no bondage but that which was chosen out of love and in liberty.

The process remains unfinished. Sometimes I think I am sure only of "What I do *not* want to do with my life," and haven't yet discovered "What I really *want* to do." But that is not entirely true. There is a sense in which I am "out of the ministry" as it is culturally and institutionally perceived. As I touch my heart's deepest desires and glimpse, even vaguely, my real giftedness, a certainty remains that (1) I have a call, (2) there are Spirit-inspired tasks for me to do, (3) a work (ministry) which will consume much of my time and energy is shaping up ahead. I do not know all its facets. In embryo it is already mine.

There is no ministry or work or accomplishment that counts which does not flow from soundness of relationships with God. Blindnesses, resistances, misunderstandings, and doubtings of long-standing have kept my relationship with God from the depth of authenticity He calls me to. When these spiritual infirmities and malformities know His healing touch, and when His wholeness substantially replaces my crippledness in specific areas important to my usefulness, He will give me work to do. He knows when I am ready.

Moses had eighty years, Paul had fourteen, the Twelve had three and one-half, before they were thrust into their work. The "deacons" at Jerusalem (Acts 6) had seven or eight years before they were given "official responsibilities" in the church. By contrast, I began my first pastorate without taking a deep breath or a second thought when I was scarcely old enough to vote. I've been on the run ever since, with no time out to deal with some of the most fundamental questions of my life. I am awfully late, I know. But I am taking a couple of years, right here in my late forties, to see if I can get some of the noise out of my ears, in order to hear God's voice as I should have been hearing it all along.

"The world is dying without Christ while you are finding yourself," I hear my imaginary critics say.

Tell it to Jesus, who waited thirty years before commencement of His ministry—while God-only-knows-how-many died without Christ.

Can I lead anyone to life, if I cannot show in my life as well as my words what it means to live abundantly (John 10:10)? Will the blind guide not lead those who follow him into a ditch (Matt. 15:14)? Will the Pharisee, whose faith has made little or no difference in the basic value structures upon which his real responses are based, who has not faced the truth about his own self-deceitfulness, who has not learned to love, whose systematized external confession of faith has never broken his rigidity and pride, ever be able to make of his proselyte anything but "twice the child of hell" he himself is (Matt. 23:15)?

There is more to being ready than seeing the need. There is more to doing the will of God than responding to the pressures of time or the expectations of others.

CHAPTER 7

The Prisoner

> *If you hold to my teaching, you are really my disciples. Then you will know the truth, and the truth will set you free. If the Son sets you free, you will be free indeed (John 8:31–32, 36).*

To say that this story is not easy to tell is to put it so mildly as to nearly miss the truth. Telling it is one of the most difficult things I have ever done. I am afraid of being rejected by those who cannot abide the thought that a "man of God" could be so weak. I am afraid to be thought a fool by some for such flagrant self-disclosure, which may have hidden costs I will be unable to assess until after publication. I am afraid someone may misappropriate this story as a license to continue in sin. God forbid!

But another fear drives me to tell it as it is: The fear that there are many Christians—true believers in the Lord Jesus who are genuinely seeking to follow Him—who, like me, have, for too many years, been desperately lonely and in great emotional distress, each thinking that he or she is "the only one" who, as a believer, still struggles and fails so miserably against sin. Baffled by repeated defeat in areas where other Christians seem to "have the victory," these miserable strugglers are at the point of giving up. Some have already crossed that line who, upon reading such a story as mine, may be called back to Jesus.

If anyone sees himself in any part of this story and finds the faintest glimmer of hope and understanding, I will gladly risk the misunderstandings of those who are uncomfortable in the presence of weakness, sickness, or pain.

The Pride That Goes Before

Monday . . .

When Audrey and I hit a communications snag last night, I amazed myself by being able to perform with moderate self-control (if not self-giving love). Praise God for limited victory.

I was angry at her seeming inability to hear me. Until I realized it was because she was experiencing the same desperate feeling—hurting and wanting nothing so badly as to be understood.

Apart from a brief blow-up on my part, it was a profitable time of learning.

I have begun to grasp something Watchman Nee says in *A Table in The Wilderness,* October 16, about spiritual leadership:

> Apostleship has its credentials. The signs of an apostle will never be lacking where there is a true divine commission. There was abundant evidence of the genuineness of Paul's. "In nothing am I behind the very chiefest apostles," he writes in Second Corinthians 12:11-12. "Truly the signs of an apostle were wrought among you in all patience, in signs, and wonders, and mighty deeds." From this we infer that endurance is first among the proofs of spiritual power. It is the ability to endure steadfastly under continuous pressure that tests the reality of our call as the Lord's "sent ones." Patience and longsuffering with joy are to be found only in those who know what it is to be "strengthened with all power, according to the might of His glory" (Col 1:11).[1]

First among the proofs of true spiritual leadership is *patience.* Signs and wonders fall somewhere below on the priority list. The primal sign of a true man of God is that he does whatever he is empowered by God to do . . . with patience.

I am delighted to see my patience-fruit growing. Thank You, Friend. Let it mature. For the sake of the Gospel.

The Terror That Roars

Thursday . . .

I have re-read Monday's entry. I am appalled! How can a man have such good intentions, such a sense of spiritual progress, and, only a few hours later, nearly destroy everything good and positive in his life? The self-deception of which I am capable astounds me!

The evening after writing my "discoveries" concerning patience, I became for thirty-six hours the exact contradiction of all I said I was growing in.

At bedtime Audrey and I disagreed about something to do with one of the kids. It started as controlled interaction, but quickly became an angry exchange. And then, on my part, it culminated in another childish explosion of rage.

Our otherwise peaceful and secure relationship has been periodically disrupted by unpredictable and destructive outbursts of hostility (sheer madness) from me. Audrey has repeatedly forgiven these eruptions and we have gone on. For the most part, in spite of the pain they have inflicted on our relationship, I have been able to forgive myself—amazingly, scarcely able to remember between outbursts that I am ever the monster I become when repressed anger bursts from its unknown source and ravages restraint.

I have tried "everything" to deal with this ruinous behavior pattern. With deep groanings I have prayed about it. Hundreds of times I have surrendered myself to God and prayed to be "sanctified wholly." I have sought to be "baptized in the Spirit," willing to speak in tongues, if that would set me free. Reams of resolutions have been made and broken. I have chronically cultivated the habit of "daily devotions." Daily times of prayer—sometimes very early in the morning—have been set aside and observed. I have sought to counteract the problem by memorizing and repeating relevent Scripture passages. For many years I have plunged enthusiastically into small group life. I have publicly confessed my problem. I have participated in Yokefellow's "prayer therapy" groups. Audrey and I attended a Marriage Encounter Weekend. I wonder if it is even possible that, from a burning subconscious desire to get help for myself, I have led in restructuring our entire local church in order to provide a support group capable of ministering to my emotional and spiritual needs.

I have reached back into my childhood in an attempt to

get to know myself. Result: I know myself better. I know that inside the visible man there is a frightened, lonely invisible child who is certain that no one—not even God—loves him. But I cannot see that anything I have done has really changed anything. The outbursts are less frequent than in younger years, but they seem more destructive than ever.

I have been trying to visualize and respond to my wife as though Jesus Himself were coming to me in her (Matt. 25:40, 45). Good idea. She desperately wants to be treated as a "fellow-heir" (1 Pet. 3:7 NASB). I want to treat her that way. But when certain emotional dynamics are present, I still blow up. My lovely visualizations are wisps of vapor caught by the hot wind, totally inadequate to tame the dreadful monster lurking inside me.

Lately, Audrey's resilience has faded noticeably. She is less ready to keep taking it. Why should she? She wants change. And it's high time change came! Neither of us can continue endlessly playing this maddening game of "outburst-guilt-forgiveness-cover-up-and-then-do-it-all-over-again."

It seems to me (who really knows but God?) that the disastrous reactions come almost "automatically"—as though someone has accidentally pushed the secret button which sets off the TNT. The dam breaks so quickly, choice scarcely seems to enter the picture (I'm probably lying to myself). I want the vicious chain to be broken. But I seem helpless, unalterably "programmed" to self-destruct.

I feel hopeless.

I think death may be the solution. Sometimes I long for it, and in my imagination I go through the process of taking my life. But I lack courage to fulfil the fantasy. I fear for the guilt it would cause my family, and the certainty with which it would undermine my work. To die in a nice, honorable automobile crash or heart attack or brain hemorrhage would leave them with a level of pain they could handle. It might even increase the value of my work, because I would not be around to spoil it with the ugly realities of my inconsistent life!

The conviction has been born in me recently that unless there can be some sign of real progress against this destructive pattern of anger—at the very least, I need to be honest enough to resign from the ministry altogether, burn my new manuscript[2] and stop polluting Christendom with ideas that I myself cannot live out in my own home.

What can I do? I have had enough of unfulfilled resolutions, ineffective confessions, and toothless rededications—none of which has led to real change.

A resident monster controls my life. And the monster is me! All my public "goodness" and "Christlikeness" is so much rubbish. The secret reality of my life is laced with passion, hatred, bitterness, violence, and murder.

If basic change does not come, I will lose Audrey and the kids. I will lose my life, as far as its value and impact for anything good are concerned.

And I cannot seem to change!

But . . . what about the biblical promises of newness and inevitable transformation into Christ's likeness? I can quote most of them. Where is the payoff?

Tuesday I spent half the day feeling like garbage about to be thrown out; the other half rationalizing that my failure in this one area of my life does not render me worthless. God loves me and I do have value. And, at the end of the day, I went into another tirade to prove it!

The People-Helper

Wednesday, at the absolute end of my rope, I went to see Norm Wakefield, afraid to hope that he could offer any real help. I confessed the horror of my sinful patterns, insisting that this gentle Christian brother listen to the description of my angry outbursts in detail. I spread before him the frightful reality of murder I had discovered in my heart.

I know he must have been shocked. But he handled it with calm compassion. Norm is a man of the Spirit, with sound understanding of how the human personality functions. I was surprised at how insightful he was. From the base of our existing friendship he affirmed what he saw as my giftedness and value as a man. Then he added several significant perceptions:

1. Anger is nearly always rooted in fear.

2. Inside me, largely untouched by Christ's love and unaffected by anything I have tried to do about it, is a frightened little boy. This inner child sees himself as bad, unacceptable. He feels hated and he is incapable of receiving God's love because of unresolved guilt for his weaknesses, failures, and sins. He dreads rejection and feels rejected most of the time. He is terrified that something will happen to prove he is as worthless as he thinks he is.

3. Audrey, on the other hand, is self-assured. She has a positive sense of self-worth. In fact, she is so confident and self-assured that sometimes she asserts herself in ways which make the feeling child in me feel endangered. At the level of spontaneous emotional responses, I have a dread of being controlled by her. One reason my reactions are so intense is because the child within is afraid that if she gains the upper hand, my last faint vestige of personal worth will be annihilated.

4. When the fear of being controlled becomes intense enough, I respond with aggression and belligerence in a subconscious attempt either (a) to regain some form of "safe control," (b) to "drive away" the threatening person, overwhelming him by trying to scare him, or (c) to actually destroy the threatening person in order to keep from being destroyed.

5. The problem is fundamentally *my* problem. Change in the people around me will not solve it. If I felt good about myself, possessing a sound inner sense of self-worth and self-acceptance, the feeling of being emotionally drowned would not come, even if the pressures did. I need to be changed. The hidden person who sees himself as worthless must experience grace and healing.

Norm believes the "inner child" can be liberated by the *truth*. Until now he has believed a lie: That he is despicable and rejected by everyone, including Jesus. Norm wants me to consider a prayerful walk into memory, to allow the Lord to touch and heal and change my remembered perspectives on the experiences that have helped to create this emotional disability.

He is not talking about a mystical "trip into the past" to

relive it. That cannot be done. Memories have been left by past experiences, but remembering is itself a present experience and the emotions rising out of memories are present emotions. The so-called "healing of the memories" is not a "going back," but a "going into" memories that are real today. It is a process of exercising faith in Jesus to touch, heal, and change the present realities of the conscious and subconscious mind. The vehicle on which the process rides is the mind's capacity for imagination.

Quite frankly, I scarcely believe "another try" is going to work out any better than my prior attempts at solution. But I trust Norm. And I am ready to try on the basis of his faith.

Lord willing . . . next week.

An Experience of Inner Healing

FRIDAY, A WEEK LATER . . .

It's 5:25 A.M. I am alone among the sleepers.

Yesterday's meeting with Norm has left me exhausted emotionally, but with a new sense of peace. Unmistakably, Jesus has been walking around among my painful memories, touching them with His grace. When I recall today the memories dealt with yesterday, I see Him involved in those situations. His perspective on them is cleansing away the lies.

Norm gently guided me through a simple process, popularly called "healing of memories," or, more scientifically, "primal therapy." (The latter term usually describes a process much more intensive and extensive than what I experienced.) The entire experience took place in the imagination and memory banks of my own mind. However, it was not, in any sense, an imaginary experience or a fantasy. It was intensely real because memories and emotions are very real.

At Norm's suggestion, I closed my eyes, and entered one end of a long hallway leading back through my whole lifetime. Along it were doors that would open into rooms which were the setting for the happenings of my life. I was instructed to walk along the hallway until I came to a door I wished to enter.

There were doors on both sides as I began to walk the

misty corridor. I seemed also to have an overview, which enabled me to look down on each room from above. I was thus able to see what was in a room before opening the door. As the passage led past adult years and into what my imagination told me were teen-age years, there were no more doors on the right side. There were just a few on the left. I could not see the end of the hall. It was shrouded in thick darkness. I knew instinctively that there were important things in my life beyond the darkness, but I feared I might not be able to see to go on.

At last I came to a door I wished to enter. It was just before the darkness.

I walked in and sat down on a metal folding chair. It was my mother's funeral. There was nothing distinguishable in the room except my mother's casket and me—a boy of twelve years. Other people were there, but they appeared as gray, nearly shapeless shadows. None had faces. I know other people were there—I can give you the names of some of them. But in my memory-pictures they are indistinguishable. They do not speak. They hardly seem human.

There were lines of light and dark between me and the coffin of my mother. When I tried to explain the lines, I felt a longing, a reaching out to one who could not respond.

I felt absolutely alone. And I felt guilty (I could not tell Norm why). But mostly I felt alone. No one explained anything to me. No one spoke to me. No one came into my loneliness to be with me in a way that affected the loneliness. (No doubt there were attempts by people at the time to do these things. But I do not remember them. Whenever I think of the scene at Mama's funeral, I feel utterly and painfully alone.) I wept loudly as the feeling tones surrounding the memories of that occasion came freshly alive.

At Norm's suggestion I invited Jesus to come into the room. He came in and stood beside me. Immediately I felt Him put His arm around my shoulders as I sat there. He told me He would always be with me, and that He understood what I was going through. I felt stronger. I wasn't alone any more. The others in the room were still shadowy, silent, and unreal. It was as if Jesus and I were alone.

Again I wept deeply and did not try to stop.

Today, eighteen hours later, when I bring up the memory of that lonely, painful time in my life, I cannot recall it without seeing Jesus there with me—as I know He was, in fact. The truth of His presence has dispelled the lie of my aloneness.

Asked if I was ready to leave the room, I said I thought I was. At the doorway I paused, Jesus standing with me, to look again at the scene. The chair in which I'd been sitting was empty. The lines of light and dark between me and the casket were noticeably dimmed. The gray shadows were all the same. But Jesus was with me.

Starting down the passageway again, I was immediately confronted by the mass of darkness. I wasn't really afraid to enter it, but I was sure I'd be unable to see anything if I did.

"Ask Jesus to give you some light," said Norm.

I did. Immediately the blackness grayed enough so I was able to see the next door.

This door led into the last two years before Mama died.

Entering I found myself standing in the kitchen of our house in Mobridge, South Dakota.

"Where is your mother?" Norm asked.

She was in the bathroom. Praying. The door was shut but I could hear her. I could not tell what she was saying—just that her voice was very "serious" and that she was praying for me.

I felt guilty. Because I was such a bad boy that my mother had to agonize so in prayer for me. And because I was such a disappointment to her. I wept as I remembered.

Norm suggested inviting Jesus to enter the room. Again He came in and immediately stood beside me, His arm around my shoulders. He began to tell me how much He loved me. He even said He *liked* me a lot. He did not feel about me the way my mother thought He felt. He told me I was okay with Him. My mother, He said, simply did not understand. She was confused about the boy (me).

I felt peace. I felt okay.

Jesus then went into the bathroom to heal my mother. She was kneeling beside the tub, her head bowed. He took her face into His hands and lifted her chin until He was looking straight into her eyes. Then Jesus kissed Mama gently on the forehead. He talked to her about the boy. Assured her that I was not basically a bad boy. Told her that God loved me very much and that I would be all right. She need not worry about me so. Furthermore, she need not worry about my dad. He too would be all right. She could rest in Jesus' love for her and her family.

Then Jesus held her close and she felt peace. And stopped being anxious about me.

I was watching and listening from the doorway. Jesus motioned and I went to my mother. She put her arms around me and mine encircled her. We held each other and loved each other and knew that everything was all right between us. The fear of non-acceptance that neither of us had understood or wanted began to fade. For that moment, at least, it did not stand between us. I told her I forgave her, and with new understanding, she believed in me.

Truth in the Inner Chamber

THURSDAY, ONE MONTH LATER . . .

Once again, I spent the afternoon with Norm Wakefield.

I told him about the depression I was feeling, the struggle I was having with fear and resentment toward certain people who seemed to be rejecting me. He responded by reminding me that if I really felt secure in Jesus, the hurt and anger which are so much my normal response to rejection would probably be significantly desensitized.

He asked if I would like to take Jesus into the "inner chamber" of my mind to touch the "little boy inside" who is so fearful. Before, we had journied into recollection and invited Jesus to become involved in memories to heal them. But this time, he said, we will not look back, but will seek to get in touch with the present "inner feeling child," to begin liberating him from fear and loneliness.

I was instructed to close my eyes and imagine a hallway leading, this time, deep inside to where the "little boy inside" is. Norm asked me to tell him when I came to a door that would lead to the boy.

It was quite dark in the corridor. The doorways were all

shrouded in shadows. But, after a few moments, I stopped to open a darkened door.

It was a familiar cubicle that my imagination has long pictured as the residence of my frightened inner child. Within the box-like room was a small boy—myself as a child.

Norm asked me to describe the chamber.

"It's very dark and bare. The only light is the light from the open door—which scarcely penetrates the darkness."

"Is there any furniture in the room?"

"No. It is just a bare room. Not a stick of furniture."

He asked me to describe the boy.

I described a shadowy figure, almost completely hidden in darkness except for his two very large eyes—eyes wide with fear. He cowers in the shadows, afraid to show his face or form.

"Is anyone there with him?"

"No. He is completely alone."

Norm suggested that Jesus might enter the room.

It was, in my mind, as though there was a "force-field" of resistance barring Jesus' (or anyone's) entrance into the cubicle.

"What is the 'force-field'?" asked Norm.

"Fear. Unbelief. The boy can't believe Jesus will not take advantage of him."

My precise feeling was that the inner child was utterly without capability of letting Jesus come near. The battle going on inside me at that moment was intense. The man of my intellect knew that the only thing to do was to welcome the Lord. But the child of my dark feelings seemed paralyzed, numb, incapable of such a response.

Norm was wise and gentle. "The boy has been hurt badly. How many people have hurt or rejected the boy?"

Several representative names came to mind, but they were merely symbols of a vast crowd from the years of my life whom I felt had rejected me.

"As an adult Christian," I said, "I thought I had forgiven these people. I have certainly gone through the conscious process of forgiving them. But whenever I think of them, I still feel the same feelings of rejection and pain."

"It's because the inner boy still feels the rejection," Norm responded. "What can be done to let Jesus come into the room?"

I thought hard, reaching inside to touch the feelings of the child in the dark. And I could only answer, "I don't know. The boy cannot seem to let down the resistance."

"Does Jesus have the ability to break down the resistant shield and come into the room?"

"Yes, He does. And if He ever comes in, it will have to be because He wants to and does. The boy cannot let Him in."

When I looked again, it seemed that Jesus was in the room. Just inside the door. His light was driving back the darkness. The "force-field" of resistance seemed to be yielding in places. The boy could be seen more clearly in the increased light.

"Can you describe the boy, now?"

I described two large frightened eyes, glowing with fear, set in a body that was not even human. It was ugly, grotesque, repulsive. I used the words "worm" and "reptile" as Norm drew the description out of me. At last, I saw him as a nearly lifeless, hardened, crumpled-looking mass, cowering in the darkest corner of the room. "A clinker, not a boy!"

"Does Jesus love the boy?"

"My intellect tells me that He does. Everything I know about Him says He does."

My guide asked me to describe what I thought Jesus' feelings are toward the boy.

"He loves him. He accepts him even as ugly as he is."

Then it seemed as if Jesus, His light now surrounding the small, remaining dark area where the child still crouched in fear, reached out and touched the "hardened clinker" that was the child's present form.

I remembered Mark 1, where Jesus reached out and touched the diseased and ugly leper. Flesh to flesh.

"What did Jesus do to the leper?" Norm asked.

"He loved him," I said. "He cleansed and healed him. He gave him a whole new body and a new life."

"Will He do this for the boy?"

"If He did it for the leper, He can do it for the boy."

The hardened, weazened form softened a little.

"Can Jesus take the boy in His arms?"

There was still the feeling of resistance. "I want him to," I said.

At that moment, in my imagination, the light that radiated from Jesus, the light He is, completely enveloped the cowering clinker of a child. He gathered the small mass of ugliness and hardness into His arms and held him close. The only darkness remaining in the room was inside the form in Jesus' arms. And even that dark residue was gradually yielding to light.

"How does the boy feel in Jesus' arms?"

"Still afraid to depend on this. Tentative. But definitely comforted and loved."

"Is the boy changing in any way?"

"He is becoming a bit softer and a bit larger—like a raisin in water. Softening and swelling as it soaks up the surrounding moisture. He is relaxing. Not so afraid."

During the final quiet moments of meditation the boy in Jesus' arms took on increasingly human form. As I look back on that scene, several hours later, I see an older child, fully human, in Jesus' arms. He is bathed through and through with light. At peace and more secure.

Thus, more of my thoughts, imaginings, reasonings, and rememberings are being brought into captivity to Jesus Christ (2 Cor. 10:4-5). I have a new capacity to deal with things that create fear of rejection, knowing more deeply than before . . . I am His child. He holds me. He loves me.

Imagination is bringing me in touch with reality, but it is not imaginary. It is a more intimate experience of everything the Bible says Jesus is to me.

Symptoms of Healing

TUESDAY, THE FOLLOWING WEEK . . .

Yesterday was a satisfying day. I actually saw a few tangible results of the process God has been working in me.

Inner cleansing, confessing before brothers, healing of memories, more knowing surrender to God, visualizing the work of Christ in me, concentrating on the truth that He knows, yet loves the real person I am—all these have combined to produce what seem to be genuine evidences of positive change and spiritual growth.

Two recent incidents illustrate this for me.

1. Saturday I went to see Bobby play basketball. Frank and Angela came in and sat a few rows below me on the bleachers. They invited me to come sit with them.

Frank is one whom I felt had rejected me. They left the church about three years ago—and I have interpreted that as rejection. Since then, each time I have seen him I have felt his disapproval of me. And with the pain always came resentment. Angela has never communicated rejection to me, but whenever I have seen her, I have felt Frank's . . . along with the accumulated pain of dozens of other church attritions.

But as we sat in the bleachers chatting about our families and various church people, I felt none of the old rejection and no resentment. I felt comfortable with them, able to accept them fully. And they seemed genuinely glad to see me.

It seemed a sign of healing.

2. Yesterday I came home proudly waving a check for this year's royalties from *Brethren, Hang Loose*. I was feeling good about myself. My book had sold more than two hundred copies per month in its sixth year since publication! Neither Audrey nor I were aware that with my lighthearted display of this check I was actually fishing for maternal approval again.

She was preoccupied with anxiety about our financial future (which for a variety of reasons looks rather uncertain at the present). "It's not enough to build a house," was her offhand comment.

I was hurt. Angry. That she would not give me the affirmation I was fishing for. After all, could she not see how this check was tangible proof of my worth? She had "put me down," I retorted, at the very point where I was feeling I had succeeded, by reminding me of problems I have not yet solved. (She had no such intent, but it is what my fearful childish ears heard.)

At that point, however, I became aware of what was happening. I was "at the breast" again, begging for "mother" to build my little ego, pat my little head and say, "My, you are such a good boy, Bobby!" I was back at the old pre-adolescent game of depending on someone else for my sense of value. Refusing to accept responsibility for my own attitudes.

As I admitted these things to myself, I also remembered *her* insecurity in the face of our real financial uncertainties.

I said to myself, "I am not going to let this happen. I'm going to take responsibility for myself. I understand her insecurity. I am not going to expect her to meet my neurotic emotional need. I'm going to make the choice to feel good about myself and I am not going to be angry."

To her I announced my intent to be responsible for my own attitudes.

This "minor" happening was, to me, major evidence that real healing is taking place inside. For it was a forthright departure from a long-standing negative pattern.

Because Jesus lives in me, loves and accepts me just as I am, and holds me close to His bosom, I have every reason to feel secure. I can allow other people to be who they are without perpetually leaning on them for approval and affirmation. I possess, in potential, in my relationship with Jesus and His with me, all I need to maintain a healthy sense of worth and hope.

To Be Continued

No, I have not yet come to the end of my stored-up fear and anger. More "inner healing" is indicated. But I seem to be getting some "handles" to work with. I have a clearer understanding of the fundamental conditioning behind certain "besetting sins." I am more in touch with primal feelings which have been programming my responses. I am *seeing* Jesus involved in my secret inner war; and He is winning (Gal. 5:17). My faith is beginning to reach nearer the depths of the wounds which have shaped my fears. Sin's ruin goes deep. But even deeper goes His grace (Rom. 5:20).

Earlier, I spoke of past attempts to deal with my seemingly

bottomless reservoir of hostility. Some of those things were, for me, essential steps in the process of grappling with the real issue. For instance, prayer, when it was honest and genuine, not merely a performance, has brought me in touch with grace. (And who is to say that the healing I am now beginning to experience is not in answer to some of those early mixed-up, earnest prayers?) Memorized Bible verses still emerge to remind me of truth and good news. Multiplied rededications may have helped establish a disposition toward surrender. Christian group life in various forms has opened me to myself, kept me aware that God is at work, and revealed the support available in God's people. Public confession has broadened the circle of accountability and involved more people in praying for my restoration. Admittedly, vast confusion beclouded some of my earlier attempts to find deliverance, and it could be argued that a few even impeded my spiritual and emotional growth. Nonetheless, God is able to use "all things" in His process of reshaping the character of His beloved (Rom. 8:28–29).

Experiences of "inner healing" like those described here have been important parts of a scheme that is bringing about the complete dismantling of my internal barriers to God. The Holy Spirit never lets up in pursuit of a clean-sweep of the entire ugly residue of sin's rape. I cannot yet announce full deliverance. But these experiences have certainly exposed realities in my life which will require the further acts of God. They have increased my capacity to appropriate God's provisions for the most difficult conflicts of my life. New habits of response are being developed which flow from internalized faith and spiritual integrity on the subconscious as well as the conscious level.

CHAPTER 8

I Took My Death Wish to the Cemetery Today

> *It greatly displeased Jonah, and he became angry. And he prayed to the Lord and said, . . . "O Lord, please take my life from me, for death is better to me than life" (Jonah 4:1–3 NASB).*

I took my "death wish" to the cemetery today. And there, amid granite grave markers and plastic flowers, was death.

Weeping willows drooped and rustled in gentle wind—they were alive. Frogs made lively leaps into a deathless "man-made" pond. Both willows and amphibians lived their fragile lives unaware that death was so near on every side.

I felt alone and out of place.

I had just said, "My life is over!" And so it seemed at the moment. Faced with deadly sickness in my soul and spirit, I was sure I could not go on living another day. My world seemed on the verge of utter collapse. All I had worked for was about to slip through my defeat-numbed fingers.

The stark and dreadful reality of my inner sickness mingled with the melody of a worship song coming from somewhere inside me—mocking my true emptiness and faithlessness with a ghostly irony. Hope—dashed again and again by my "uncontrollable," angry, sinful outbursts—seemed dead and gone.

"There is no more hope!" I had bitterly sobbed.

So, I came here, to this place, to see if I could get a perspective on the death for which I had been so earnestly praying. And sure enough, death was here.

All whose buried earthly tents lie around me now, are in

the process of being forgotten. If, like me, any of them ever hoped that his death would emphasize his existence, or would underscore his cries for help, or would gain him the sympathy, concern, or notice he felt he lacked in life—if, somewhere, he is conscious, he now knows that death accomplished *none of those things!* It may have come as a shock, a deep grief, or a relief to the living left to deal with his memory. But it was not emphasis, nor the filling of some lack. Death was just . . . the end. The beginning of the process of being forgotten. As years go by, both the pain and joy in knowing "our dear departed" will become enhazed in the blurry banks of increasingly distant memory. Soon, no one will even mention his name.

Is that good or bad? Is that what I have been wishing for? Does my heart really desire the inevitable anonymity of the "departed"?

Written in a cemetery
near Scottsdale, Arizona, in 1978.

CHAPTER 9

The Incredible Hope

> *Surely He has borne our griefs—sickness, weakness and distress—and carried our sorrows and pain . . . and with the stripes that wounded Him we are healed and made whole (Isa. 53:4–5 Amplified Bible).*

What joy it is to have hope!

It is reason to live and not die. It is life-and-breath-giving light piercing gloomiest darkness, supplying stability to rubbery knees, brightness to tear-clouded eyes, comfort to pain.

I have experienced the gnawing agony of hopelessness—when the only thing to dissuade me from taking my miserable life was the dread of death itself. Those were days when I thought I had tried everything to deal with my inner sickness, and was sure the rest of my life could only be a living hell. My spiritual eyes were blind. I could not see the hope that oozes from page after page of Scripture.

"We are saved in hope!" cries Paul, as he tells how all creation waits for our unveiling as true children of God—an unveiling guaranteed by the promises and workings of God in our lives (Rom. 8:17–30).

"And let us rejoice and exult in our hope of experiencing and enjoying the glory of God," he exhorts (Rom. 5:2 Amplified).

And now I see it. He has taken the scales from my self-focused eyes, and has kindled in my discouraged heart the brightly burning hope that *I will be whole.*

Healing stands out among the many attractive provisions of

the Promise of the Gospel. From prophecy (Isa. 53:4–5) to historicity (Matt. 8:16–17) Christ's ministry is reported to involve full cure of "all sicknesses"—including every human malady from fever to evil spirits.

Paul, in his letters, repeatedly lifts the gaze of his readers to the zenith of healing's hope . . .

> May God himself, the God of peace, sanctify you through and through. May your whole spirit, soul and body be kept blameless at the coming of our Lord Jesus Christ. The one who calls you is faithful and he will do it (1 Thes. 5:23–24).

When can I expect God's wholeness to displace my suffusive, adhesive sickness?

Paul sometimes speaks in terms which make it seem that the answer is "Soon. Very soon." For the apostle to the Gentiles was possessed of a most astonishing hope:

> I want to know Christ and the power of his resurrection and the fellowship of sharing in his sufferings, becoming like him in his death, and so, somehow, to attain to the resurrection from the dead (Phil. 3:10–11).

To which the Amplified Bible adds:

> . . . even while in the body!

Could human hope in Christ really be that radiant, that big? Does he dare to think that it might be possible for the perfecting benefits of the resurrection to burst into human experience in the earthly lifetime of a believer? Dare he suggest that resurrection's full restoration of God's image and experiential deliverance from the last and deepest effects of sin are possible for a Christian still living his temporal human life?

It seems incredible. And this is not the only place he talks like this. See Romans 6:4–9; 8:11; 8:28–30; Second Corinthians 3:18; 4:10–14.

Has Paul obtained this grace? No.

> Not that I have already obtained all this, or have already been made perfect, but I press on to take hold of

that for which Christ Jesus took hold of me. Brothers, I do not consider myself yet to have taken hold of it. But one thing I do: Forgetting what is behind and straining toward what is ahead, I press on toward the goal to win the prize for which God has called me heavenward in Christ Jesus (Phil. 3:12-14).

Nor does he suggest the names of anyone else he knows who has done so.

There is for the believer no real boundary between the eternal-heavenly world and temporal-earthly world. It is merely a matter of "seeing." We are, even now, "seated . . . with him in the heavenly realms in Christ Jesus" (Eph. 2:6). Could we see with fully opened spiritual eyes, we would find ourselves with Him *now*, battling beside Him *now*, in the great heavenly conflict (Eph. 6:10-18), fully clothed in Him *now* (Gal. 3:26-27), and completely fulfilling His purpose for us *now* (Eph. 1:3-14).

God's plan is a single plan. He doesn't have a high plan for heaven and a low plan for earth. Temporal and earthly are eternally bound with heavenly and spiritual (Eph. 1:9-10).

Under the baton of the Mastar Conductor, we are playing the opening (temporal) movement of an everlasting symphony. What we are living through and experiencing now is not irrelevent and useless stuff to patiently endure while waiting for death to launch our true destiny. The present stuff of the believer's life is the stuff of eternity and the resurrection. Glory is not all future.

Now—at the present moment . . .

> We, who with unveiled faces all reflect the Lord's glory, are being transformed into his likeness with ever-increasing glory, which comes from the Lord, who is the Spirit (2 Cor. 3:18).

In the future . . .

> Dear friends, now we are children of God, and what we will be has not yet been made known. But we know that when he appears, we shall be like him, for we shall see him as he is. Everyone who has this hope in him purifies himself, just as he is pure (1 John 3:2-3).

God's single, ultimate aim for us, the climactic crescendo toward which the symphony is moving from the first movement to the finale, is this: *That we may become forever and in every way like Jesus* . . . including all that is involved in resurrection from the dead, toward which we are to be stretching as though we expected to reach it in our earthly lifetime.

Don't talk to me of waiting until death to be healed and free. Don't glibly point to my emotional pain, neurotic guilt, besetting sins, and internal damage and ask me to just "take it." God is at work now to bring into my life all the benefits of redemption. He has not said "Later" about very many things. As I become ready to know Christ (at the deepest depths of my person) and to experience Him (at the level of truest reality) I can make authentic progress toward the prize.

Wholeness and healing at the level I need will not come with merely mouthing Bible verses. It will not come through glib prayers spoken like pagan incantations over a closed mind and deceitful heart unwilling to know and face truth in the innermost part (Ps. 51:6). But when I am ready to be known, and I am determined to be healed at whatever cost to ego or image, I can pursue health and expect to obtain it (Matt. 7:7–11).

An Aggressive Pursuit of Healing

In sharing in mid-pursuit from my own stretch for the prize, I am not suggesting that the people or methods God is using to restore me are the ones He intends to use universally. I think there are important universal insights and principles to be drawn from my experience as illuminated by the Word of God. But our infinite Father is not only "able to do immeasurably more than all we ask or imagine, according to His power that is at work within us" (Eph. 3:20), but at His disposal are "all things" which He will use by the Holy Spirit to bring us to the through-and-through wholeness for which His plan calls (Rom. 8:28–29). His methods are as varied as His many-sided wisdom (Eph. 3:10) and His absolute knowledge of persons (John 2:25; 1 Cor. 13:12).

After a few, scattered, "healing of the memories" experiences, with Norm Wakefield and others, my life continued its day-in-day-out trek. There were a few positive results from "going inside" to deal with volatile issues lying below the surface. But day-by-day living soon revealed that I had merely rippled the surface of the internal damage. Conflicts came. The old dynamite was set off again.

But this time there was a difference. I had caught a fleeting glimpse of the truth behind the eruptions. I knew those secret forces were not untouchable. I had seen the tiniest tip of a great iceberg of "truth in the innermost part" and I knew there was much more to understand and apply to my emotional/volitional life. I had breathed just enough hope to think that God's grace could reach more deeply in me than it was reaching—that the possibility exists (even though it often has seemed quite faint) that change could come at as deep a level in my life and mind and emotions as was necessary to set me truly free. A couple of pictures had been straightened on the wall of my inner life, and I liked the look of it. It made me ready to consider contracting for some in-depth, broad scale interior renovation.

God, as is His wont, busied Himself in my life, arranging circumstances to provide a scenario so full of trauma that I was forced to keep facing my primal disarray. In this book I've detailed some of His providential "arranging." There were times when the internal chaos seemed so great that I felt more hopeless than before. But then the wind of the Spirit within would brood over the emotional rubble to gently fan the flicker of hope which had been ignited.

I had been reading Cecil Osborne, *The Art of Learning to Love Yourself:*

> We now know experientially that nothing is ever lost, nothing completely forgotten. Waiting to be recalled are the memories of all that has ever happened to us. The erosion of the years does not destroy any experience or event: the infant screaming for his bottle, the anguish of being born, the embarrassment experienced on that first date, the panic of being left at kindergarten, the shame of being ridiculed by other children, or the uncounted nights of terror when left alone in a dark room. The mind is an incredibly sensitive photographic plate on which

everything has been recorded with infinite fidelity. A very few of these memories are available to recall. More than ninety-nine out of a hundred childhood memories, with all the feelings surrounding them, are filed away in the unconscious mind.

But unlike pictures filed away in a cabinet, these thousands of pain-laden memories are exerting profound influence on our lives today. They color our attitudes, and distort our ideas. Every adult relationship is in some degree affected by these childhood experiences and the primal pain that colors them.[1]

In this book and others (i.e., *Release from Fear and Anxiety*[2]) this noted Christian counselor, co-founder of the Yokefellow program, describes an intensive form of "healing of the memories" for which he claims phenomenal results. The process is called "Primal Integration Therapy." Osborne discovered it several years ago, before he was familiar with the term "Primal Therapy." Though he had had no previous experience with this method, following an inner urge (he "felt led"[3]) he guided a therapy group member into expression of some hitherto unexpressed feelings.

I had her do some deep breathing for several minutes, then regressed her to childhood and told her to float around for a bit between ages three and six. By utilizing some other techniques since refined through thousands of hours of experience, she was triggered into a series of ear-splitting screams. She directed them at her mother first: rage, fear, indignation, pain, hate. This placid, frozen-faced young woman suddenly became a feeling person for the first time in her life . . . When her rage at mother seemed exhausted, she began to scream at daddy, only now it was a mixture of hurt and a longing for a daddy to love her, cuddle her, talk to her. She continued until she was completely exhausted. Then she began to sob almost uncontrollably. These were primal sobs, in the voice of a little girl, tears of hurt and loneliness she had never been allowed to shed, for crying was as great a sin as anger in her home.

"What a relief it was to get those screams and tears out at that first session," she said. "I knew there was much more down there, and it did come out in later private sessions, but I had never experienced such relief in my entire life as I did when I was allowed to scream my anger and hurt. I knew right then that I could get rid of all those pills I was living on." Ultimately she was able to function without her tranquilizers and antidepressants.

Subsequently she had between forty and fifty hours of individual therapy, letting out the accumulated pain of her thirty-two years. Seven years of rather intensive "talk therapy" had been able to accomplish little more than stabilizing her as an emotionally depressed robot.[4]

After following the initial inner urge, and seeing the potential for healing which lay in this simple formula, Osborne found scientific affirmation of his discoveries in the writings of Arthur Janov. The significant difference between Janov and Osborne rests in the fact that Janov is convinced that belief in God is merely another neurosis, and therefore, unnecessary or even harmful. Osborne, on the other hand, is an evangelical Christian who understands that the relationship with God is an authentic personal relationship which often needs healing, along with other relationships which may be dealt with in Primal Therapy.

Two people in our church, a man and his wife, had each completed forty hours of Primal Therapy, with positive results. As they shared their experience, I began to wonder if I should take my bundle of pain and expose it to this strange, somewhat frightening process.

I had many misgivings. Who was the therapist who would guide the process? Was he a born-again Christian? Was this procedure in keeping with basic biblical principles? Would the process tamper with my faith? Were there dangers involved in "going outside the body of Christ" to pursue inner healing? What will people think of me? What will I think of myself?

Two church families who believed in me and knew about my need for inner healing saw the potential of Primal Integration Therapy and provided the funds for an initial forty hours.

As I drove to the first session, I was shaking with fear. Not all my misgivings had been satisfied. So much was unknown.

A sense of great need mingled with a sort of "last-ditch hope" had moved me to make the appointment.

"God, I'm scared," I said aloud, as I picked my way through morning traffic. Inside I felt like jelly.

Just moments before arrival at the therapist's office, I turned on the car radio and punched the button tuned to one of the local religious stations. Just in time to catch the last line of the last chorus of the song the Back to the Bible Hour Quartet was singing:

". . . God will take care of you!"

I heard nothing else until I arrived at my destination. For I was hearing the voice of my God personally speaking peace to my anxious spirit in the words of a single lyrical line, telling me He would be with me every moment of the ordeal which lay ahead.

Primal Integration Therapy may be perceived differently by others who have been through the process. My experience leads me to describe it thus: It is an intensive process by which one is helped to get in touch with unresolved emotional pain which lies below the level of consciousness, to experience this pain on the conscious level, and to trace the painful emotions to their roots. The person can then understand and resolve the inner emotional issues which continue to shape personal attitudes and responses. The ultimate purpose of the process is to bring inner healing and restoration of personal sovereignty (freedom of choice). Under God, for me, it has been a means of tearing away barriers to love and freedom. It became a setting for dealing with sin, forgiveness, cleansing, and surrender to God at a deeper level than I ever thought possible.

Primal Therapy is not hypnotism. None is involved. There was never any sense that I was somehow giving control of my mind to someone else. I was always, ultimately, in control of the process. I was fully aware of the present, of where I was and what I was doing, even while intensely engaged in the process of "reliving" past experiences and emotions. The painful feelings which surfaced were actually there, inside me. They were real. And they were mine. Most were bound to specific memories, actual happenings in my life.

The conclusions I was encouraged to draw from these intensive sessions and the choices those conclusions have eventually led to, were my own, based on new knowledge of myself and a fresh grasp of the truth. I was always left free to form conclusions which, in a few cases, were different from those of the therapist. He was present to help me find my own way to self-discovery and resolution of the inner conflicts.

There was never any attempt to tamper with my faith or theology or value system.

In the midst of the therapy I was keenly aware of God's presence and activity. Again and again, even at the most intensive moments in the process, I would find myself praying over some new insight as it burst into the light. I was able to read very little except the Bible, which began to speak to me in fresh and expansive ways. An unbeliever might gain from the primal process in terms of personal healing, even without a personal relationship with God. But as a believer, I found it a tremendous time of spiritual cleansing, a revelation of the truth about my hidden sin and the sin of humankind, and a significant opportunity to receive God's forgiveness, salvation, and healing. The resulting freedom is increasingly becoming freedom to love God and to grow up in my relationship with Him, and to love and grow up in my relationships with those near me.

In my journal, I recorded significant aspects of my Primal Integration experience. I include here only one entry. It will doubtless leave many questions unanswered, but seems the best way to bring the reader quickly inside the process.

Cutting the Cord

Last evening's session in "the PIT"[5] seems to have been most significant in terms of establishing the direction of my life away from neurotic dependence on others, toward "the right sort of independence" (James 1:4 Phillips).

The session began with a series of deep breaths.

"Deeper and deeper . . . sinking down, sinking down." Therapist Dirk Yow's gentle voice intoned familiar words.

Then, as breathing became long and deep, I was told to let a moan escape my lips with the next breath.

"O-o-o-o-oh!" I complied in a ghostly groan.

"Let the pain out," Dirk instructed.

Even after more than thirty hours of Primal Therapy, there was still pain there. I felt it. I had been aware of it before I came into this session. A deep unhappiness, the underlying depression and dissatisfaction which has always been the emotional backdrop of my life.

As my "O-o-o-oh!" intensified to a deep wail of inner sadness and pain, I was consciously aware of no specific incident connected with it. It was just there. So much a part of what I am, so familiar, so natural—an inner agony I have never been without as far back as memory takes me.

So I groaned and wailed in touch with the pervasive pain —intent on finding some way to express an inexpressible inner sorrow. No words came. But its throbbing reality could not be denied. The cry, the wail, the moan, the sobbing and weeping were my vehicles of expression—"inner groanings which cannot be uttered" were finding expression in a wordless scream.

I felt Dirk's hands on my head, spreading his fingers firmly over and down my scalp. My crying intensified, in shorter bursts now. A series of childish outcries of pain.

"Let your body do whatever it wants to do," he instructed.

I began to pound the pad with my fists as each cry left my body. I found myself kicking my legs and writhing in some deep physical struggle. Almost a life-or-death struggle.

"Push!" the therapist shouted.

Instinctively, without remembering (for no conscious memories remain of the event) I knew where I was and what the struggle was all about. I was in my mother's womb—in the very throes of the birthing process. My conscious mind understood where I was and what was going on, but from inside, the anguish I felt was still without words.

I pushed and kicked and twisted and beat down with my fists, as though if I were to lie still at this moment I would surely die there in the opening of the womb.

"Push harder!" shouted Dirk above the sound of my primal outcries. "You'll never get out if you don't!"

The sense of entrapment which has surfaced so often

during these intensive sessions came again. It's a helpless feeling I've consciously had through most of my adult life. At that point, I began to make some important "connections."[6] Namely: If I am, emotionally, still in the womb of my mother, my prenatal attachment to any degree unbroken, my weaning unfinished, it explains the problems I am having in several other relationships—I can see how I have also functioned as though I were in the womb of my wife and of other women who have had a significant role in my life. And, further, there are a number of *men* to whom I have clung in neurotic dependence. In fact, I think I see the same "in-the-womb" pattern in my responses to some of the institutions in which I have been associated—i.e., my denomination, my academic *alma mater,* and Our Heritage Church.

After a lengthy period of intensive primal struggle and crying, trying to plumb the depths of my hitherto nameless inner pain, sure that I was actually reliving the emotional experience of my birth (which for the about-to-be-born, is often a wordless moment of intense trauma) I felt Dirk's hands under my shoulders. Grabbing me by the upper arms he was physically dragging me upward on the pad. At first I thought it was to protect me from kicking the wall. But he did not stop when my head reached the edge. He kept pulling.

"What is he doing?" I puzzled. Then I started pushing with my legs to help in whatever the process was.

By the time my shoulders were off the pad, touching the carpeted floor, I was back in the opening of my mother's womb, being pulled out of the womb and into the world of separation from my mother's body.

There was a great sense of relief as my feet followed the rest of my body out onto the floor . . . and I lay there, still.

Lying there, near exhaustion, relaxed, the desperate struggle behind me, I saw that all my life I have lived as though I were still part of my mother—and extension of her. I have adopted the same style with Audrey and others—functioning in many ways as extensions of them. Part of me has directed inordinate amounts of energy toward trying to do what would please these people, and unconsciously, what would please my mother. I have evaluated myself by her criteria and felt about myself what I perceived as her feelings about me. I have made major decisions in my life (i.e., life's work, marriage, and so on) in line with what might please Mama . . . as though I were still attached to her by the uncut umbilical cord!

I gave Mama many faces after her death, in the persons of people to whom I unconsciously responded as I would to her. And people on whom I unconsciously projected my unhealed childish perception of her feelings.

My sense of entrapment is related to the fact that another part of me has longed for "the right sort of independence" which is inherent in normal growth toward mature manhood. My unflagging sense of weakness and inferiority grow out of this continuing infantile dependency. In important aspects of my life I have continued to respond and feel like "Mama's little boy," long after I should have fully assumed manhood. When I "married my mother" (which I did in Audrey) it was "natural" that I would unwittingly become "Audrey's little boy." And there are others with whom I have assumed the same ridiculous dependent role. (This does not describe the normal, healthy side of these relationships, only the side which has caused the pain.)

Dirk then guided me into additional procedures to set the truth more firmly in my mind and emotions: i.e., intensive repetition of the confession (repetition until I actually *felt* the impact of what I was saying) . . .

"Mama, I'm not part of you any more!"

"I'm not your little boy any more!"

"I'm free from you!"

. . . Each repeated with the thudding emphasis of the bataca.[7]

Later, I was guided in a tender affirmation of personal value as an individual, apart from the ersatz sense of value offered from others on whom I make myself dependent.

To live in this new, grown-up world I am building for myself is both an exciting prospect and a difficult undertaking. Old fears and habits are so deeply imbedded. To one degree or another, all my most important personal relationships are set up according to life-in-the-womb. In order to align my life with truth I'm now seeing, every one of these relationships will necessarily undergo change—in some cases, painful change. I am afraid I will go "too far" in my quest for living in the new liberty and, thus, needlessly hurt some of my most valuable relationships. But I also have the opposite fear: That I will not go far enough. That I will be unable to change my patterns of weakness and dependency and will stop short of the liberty for which I have been set free. And so all the hopes gained in "the PIT" will become part of that old bitter stockpile of unrealized promises and dreams.

I have yet another fear: That the things in my life I am now identifying as "Mama's things" may, some of them, actually be "God's things." And not knowing the difference, I may do damage to my relationship with God. The Word and the Spirit will have to guide me in the selection process. It will be worth the risk. After all, "It is for freedom that Christ has set us free" (Gal. 5:1).

All fears aside, I have a new sense that I have indeed *experienced* my birth. And the experience has set in my heart the truth that *I was born to be a separate and distinct and unique individual from my mother and everyone else.* I am never to be merely an "extension" of another person. I, as the person I am, have intrinsic worth that is my own.

No one "owns" me, except the God revealed in Jesus. I have freedom to *choose* to bind myself to others in relationship, commitment, submission, love, servanthood, giving, self-sacrifice. But it is to be strictly *voluntary*. Nothing is to be expected of me simply because I was born in or broken to some lesser role than the others in my life.

It is not a matter of carnal pride, but of honest, proper, rightful self-esteem based on the fact that I am a person. I was personally created by God, I was born, the umbilical cord was cut, and I am therefore a unique person of at least equal value to anyone else in my life. I possess God-granted autonomy, freedom, and independence. And nothing is legitimate or right or holy which denies to me any of these realities.

The Use of Psychological Method in the Church

Many times I have questioned the validity of the process I have been pursuing. Where, in Scripture, did anyone ever need to take the Minnesota Multi-Phasic personality inventory to get to know himself? Why, when the New Testament Church's simple life together in the Spirit was so powerful in transforming people from rebels to lovers of God and man, would the church today, in touch with the same Holy Spirit, need the help of a psychologist or of extra-biblical psychological therapies in order to cure its members' spiritual/emotional wounds?

I see at least two possible answers.

First, the state of the church. The Holy Spirit has His ways of bringing needed personal revelations-leading-to-healing to those who are listening for His voice and are part of a healthy, functioning church family. The church family envisioned in Scripture could offer the kind of loving confrontation and acceptance, in an atmosphere of honesty, transparency, and caring that would allow body members to know and be themselves, encourage them to be honest in dealing with their emotions and provide them with healthy, visible models to follow in the pursuit of wholeness. The benefits of testing and expression of basic (primal) emotions would be inherent in the lifestyle of this kind of church, rendering the need for psychological inventories and therapies void. But most of us did not grow up in a church like that. And there is a perilous lack of models of such a life-together.

Second, the state of the Christian mind. The scarcity of healthy spiritual models—personal and corporate—has left most Christians confused about discipleship and largely unemancipated from the world and its wisdom. While we were not looking, the Enemy sneaked in and sowed tares among the wheat in our approach to many of the basic issues of life. The culture in which we live has been shaped and reshaped by layer upon layer of philosophy and psychology—man's best attempts to bring order into his chaotic rebel life. Christians, in turn, with few visible models which truly demonstrate the Gospel's alternative culture, have been shaped by the secular culture.

But can it be right (or even possible) for us to use such "secular" things as personality testing, psychological counseling, or emotional therapies, to bring the people of God into harmony with purposes of God they are missing? My personal belief-system argues that God Himself has provided us—in His Word, His Son, His Spirit, and His Body—all that is needed to bring release from the world's strangle hold. But my belief-system is, by conscious commitment, based on the revelation of the Bible. And discovered in the Bible, upon closer examination, are several incidents in which God used persons or movements outside the church, operating in line with His principles (often unconsciously) to accomplish His purpose. One example is the way He used that succession of Old Testament conquerors to bring Israel to repentance. Another example, this one relating to healing, involves that unorthodox non-disciple, in Mark 9:38-40, who was succeeding in casting out evil spirits in Jesus' name—and Jesus approved of His healing work, even though the man was not a follower of Jesus in the strictest sense.

Truth is reality. Much reality is visible and, according to Romans 1:18-20, even knowledge leading toward faith in and worship of God can be gained by observation of the natural world, completely apart from exposure to the biblical revelation. The discovery of truth by observation of what is visible will, in many ways, be incomplete and insufficient, but what is true is true, however it is discerned.

If the church, because of its saturation by the world, its captivity to human tradition, its ignorance or prejudice or fear or pride, is blind to certain facets of truth which can set it free, is it unthinkable that God may, if He chooses, open up the hidden areas using extra-biblical disciplines—such as science, medicine, or psychology—which seek to draw truth from observation of mankind and/or the created universe? Truth, or insight into truth, gleaned from or stimulated by these faulty human vehicles must, of course, be tested by the Word of God (2 Tim. 3:16-17) and by the anointing of the Spirit (1 John 2:20), to see that it is truly consistant with divine revelation. It should be assumed that, coming from a source outside biblical revelation, all such insight or truth *will indeed be incomplete* and will need to be sharpened against the pure whetstone of revelation in order to be made truly true.

Some kinds of healing and some kinds of change cannot come without help. But, as it exists in most places today, the church cannot offer the kind of support its members need to move toward wholeness in certain important areas. New structures are needed—both corporate and personal. So, much aware of the risks involved and the need to align all extra-biblical insights to the light of Scripture, we may borrow, for a time, a structure (such as a personality test or therapy group) to learn how to make progress toward health. Ultimately the "borrowed" structure must be changed or replaced to conform to the biblical norm, and the "borrowed" truth must become totally absorbed in a mature knowledge of God's mind. We must keep searching the Word to learn the pure way God intends for this insight or healing process to be integrated into the mainstream of body life. It may be that, as time passes, all that is left in the church of the "borrowed" truth or method, are living models of changing lives and/or a more complete understanding of how to help each other grow. The borrowed structures will disappear altogether, as their functions are integrated into the life of the church.

Conclusions from "The PIT"

Primal Integration Therapy dealt with burning spiritual issues in my life with which the church—even the fresh, transparent, loving body of which I am a part—was not prepared to deal effectively. This group was prepared to love me, free me to face my sickness, stand by me in my weakness and failure, encourage me to press my quest for inner healing, and pay the high cost of expert care. They could see the need, they prayed powerful, persistent, and believing prayers, and some seemed willing to lay down their lives for me. But my need was too deep for the resources the church—even this comparatively healthy church—had available within itself. It was necessary to go "outside."

Frankly, I know of no church that possesses the skills, understanding, and confidence to deal with serious emotional sickness at the level at which it must be confronted if fundamental change is to come. And yet, all the problems dealt with in the primal healing process are *spiritual* problems—sin, guilt, forgiveness, hate, anger, estrangement, fear, loneliness, disorientation, self-destruction, cleansing, freedom, and so on. Spiritual problems are problems the living church is uniquely authorized and empowered by its Head to confront (Matt. 10:8; 18:15-20; Mark 16:15-18; Luke 10:9; John 20:23).

When the church is fulfilling the dreams of its Head and Savior, I am convinced, it will be able to deal with basic human sicknesses and bondages with greater effectiveness and thoroughness and natural integration than the trained Primal therapist. (Until the time when these healing skills, or something more effective, are inherent in the community-life of God's people, the church will continue to need the aid of therapists and other professional people-helpers to do what it is not free to do.) I believe the Holy Spirit is now at work changing the church until it fulfills the Lord's full vision. Perhaps we will, even in this generation, see congregations which become visible models of the powerful healing community the church will be when Christ presents her to Himself "radiant . . . without stain or wrinkle or any other blemish, but holy and blameless" (Eph. 5:27).

I became keenly aware, as the painful processes of Primal Therapy ensued, that what I was dealing with was sin and its effects in my person—my own sin (set in concrete in my personality before I understood repentance and cleansing), the sins of the most significant others in my life, and the sins of society. This was not "surface sin." I had learned to deal with that through confession and acceptance of God's ever-offered forgiveness. What confronted me now was the sin-damage, the inner spiritual ruination behind most of my surface sin. Never have I had such a sense of the saturation of my entire being with evil and its havoc. I dug around among the roots of my most destructive habits. I saw in me things I had convinced myself were no longer part of my life as a Christian. But there they were, alive and kicking in the present reality of my inner being—hate, jealousy, murder, bitterness, fear of hell—the whole tribe of angry rebels against the mind of God!

I knew all was forgiven—the old and recent, the known and

unknown—and that I stood justified by faith in Jesus Christ. This meant I could confront the inner structures of evil without guilt, and that, even though I would discover some pretty ugly attitudes and feelings lurking there, I need not fear condemnation (Rom. 8:1). My salvation was never in doubt.

Sometimes, acting upon early teaching, I had claimed full inner cleansing "by faith" (which, I fear, was more wishful thinking than genuine faith). But still, His cleansing had never reached these primal structures of sin in my subconscious life. Wholeness, for me, has waited for understanding and faith to touch the dispositional roots.

The kind of healing that can bring order to this primal chaos seems to demand certain processes that are largely missing from the life of the typical church. However, the Scriptures seem to provide for and promise the benefits available in these processes.

The Scriptures encourage expression of negative primal feelings. Expression of intense emotions as anger, resentment, rage, hate, fear, discouragement, depression, sorrow, remorse, bitterness, bewilderment, and a host of other feelings, is met with complete acceptance in the Holy Scriptures—especially in the Psalms. The Psalms comprise the original hymnbook of the people of God, intended to be sung as an act of worship to God. I cannot imagine the typical pious evangelical congregation gathering on Sunday morning, all wearing their best clothes and faces, lifting as *worship* a hymn calling for vengeance on someone. But note the lyrics of this sacred hymn:

> Appoint a wicked man over him;
> And let an accuser stand at his right hand.
> When he is judged, let him come forth guilty;
> And let his prayer become sin.
> Let his days be few;
> Let another take his office.
> Let his children be fatherless,
> And his wife a widow.
> Let his children wander about and beg;
> And let them seek sustenance far from their ruined homes.
> Let the creditor seize all that he has;

And let strangers plunder the product of his labor.
Let there be none to extend lovingkindness to him,
Nor any to be gracious to his fatherless children.
Let his posterity be cut off;
In a following generation let their name be blotted out.
(Ps. 109:6–12 NASB).

A worthy hymn to be sung by saints!

This is but one example of the so-called "Deprecatory Psalms." Before its last song is sung the "Original Hymnbook" gives the original believers a spiritual vehicle for expressing the whole range of intense emotions. And it all has God's blessing!

God never intended that we be deprived of healthy expression of our real emotions. The Scriptures clearly define legitimate and holy ways for this need to be satisfied. One of them is to get alone or to get together with other believers and wail out our true feelings, in all their ugliness and intensity before the Lord—as an act of giving our true selves (not just our "nice" selves) to Him. It is an act of worship more genuine than many of us experience in a lifetime of worship services.

In a legalistic attempt at holiness, churches and parents have taught that many emotions are "off-limits" for Christians and "good boys and girls." In response, many of us have learned to stifle, suppress, and repress a lot of sin! Instead of learning how to let it surface, face it as the sin it is, and admit the personal neediness it demonstrates. When my primal responses were being constructed I was being taught that nearly all intense emotions were sinful. So, systematically, I learned to stuff and store my anger, hatred, fear, and guilt. The church helped me to become the primal hypocrite I have become. The personal dishonesty I learned at her knee led to inner sickness so entrenched that the only way it could begin to be cured was for someone to give me freedom to express the pain that had become an emotional cancer eating my life away from the interior.

Buried pain—undisclosed, undiagnosed, unhealed—is not merely a problem of personal discomfort. It has the potential to profoundly affect one's performance as a Christian and the church's performance as a reflection of Christ. Expressed pain, on the other hand, can be brought to God for restoration.

The Scriptures teach that full inner healing from sin and its effects requires intense and extensive repentance.

Jesus' first message, inaugurating His ministry in Galilee, was a call to repentance (Matt. 4:17). The original word is *metanoia*: to be changed in the basic structures of one's life.

"Repent" is a word evangelicals use too glibly. The meanings communicated by word and rite have fallen ineffectively short of the process of total renovation of character and personality the Bible promises to those who follow Jesus. Biblical repentance is much more than a time of crying over past sins or a decision to comply with some list of surface prohibitions (i.e., no smoking, no drinking, no dancing).

The immensity of repentance's field of operation is described by Jesus in the Great Commission:

> Teaching them to *obey everything* I have commanded you (Matt. 28:20, italics added).

The intensity of repentance required to bring change to sinful inner motivations and response mechanisms is described by James:

> Submit yourselves then, to God. Resist the devil, and he will flee from you. Come near to God and he will come near to you. Wash your hands, you sinners, and purify your hearts, you double-minded. Grieve, mourn and wail. Change your laughter to mourning and your joy to gloom. Humble yourselves before the Lord, and he will lift you up (James 4:7–10).

Reading that, I remembered the scenes I witnessed at the altars of churches and camp meetings that were part of my early years. There was confusion about many things concerning God and Scripture, but the rite of sinners coming forward to weep and wail over their rebellion against God seemed to come directly out of James 4. Except that what we experienced in those moments of public contrition was merely the beginning of a process which needed to continue with expanding understanding and more penetrating honesty until every inner resistance to the mind of God is torn down and all our rebellious inner structures are transformed.

I also see in this passage an apt description of what I was experiencing in Primal Integration Therapy. The unbeliever would probably not perceive himself as dealing with sin or humbling himself before God. He would thus be missing a most important essential for mental/spiritual health. But, as a Christian, I instinctively saw myself as weeping and wailing over my sins, purifying my heart, bringing my mind to a singleness of spiritual focus, humbling myself before the Lord. Therapy sessions did not follow James' pattern exactly, but building on them, my spirit and faith could continue working with the revealed problems until the necessary spiritual transactions could take place in on-going interaction with God.

I had "repented" before. Many times, in bitter, remorseful tears. I had been deeply sorry for sins. But there were sin-issues in me that I simply had never seen. Some of the most seriously destructive had been stuffed in subconscious vaults before I knew how to deal with them. Now they were stripped bare—sin-formed and diabolical primal structures which filled my life with an insidious fifth column of pain. Now I could, by faith, experience the nearness of God in previously "closed off" areas of my personality. I could consciously receive forgiveness and cleansing as extensive as my known needs. *Metanoia,* primal change, could begin in parts of my life which, though never beyond the reach of grace, had remained beyond the reach of faith and choice.

According to the Scriptures, many people suffer from evil spirits which, to varying degrees, control their lives.

Despite the inclusion in the Gospel narrative of many case histories in which Jesus and the disciples healed people by driving evil spirits (demons) out of them, modern Christians understand little of this process, and seldom speak of it except to spiritualize the case histories. We are more comfortable thinking of evil spirits as related to voodooism or witchcraft.

I have not normally deviated from this pattern. In twenty-seven years of ministry I had seen three men and one woman (all believers) delivered from evil spirits in response to prayer (at least, I was fairly certain that that is what caused the dramatic change which took place in their lives in answer to our specific prayers). These incidents involved alcohol addiction, a consuming urge to kill, a controlling problem of lust, and intense hatred of parents. But even though there has been a constant parade through my life of others with terrible, seemingly unsolvable problems beyond their control or mine, evil spirits were usually the farthest thing from my mind as I tried to help.

But something happened to make me wonder if there is not a need to take another look at the Bible's teaching on this controversial subject. After one or two intensive sessions of Primal Therapy, I turned to the Bible for an explanation of the things I was experiencing. I discovered the truth about in-depth repentance in James and elsewhere. But I also began to see something else. Usually, when I came upon a description of someone going through something similar to what was happening to me in therapy, it was the story of someone being released from an *evil spirit*. I decided to re-read the New Testament to locate and study every recorded case history and every statement of Jesus or the apostles concerning evil spirits and deliverance from them. My personal identification with these stories was reinforced, even down to the physical responses of persons in the throes of deliverance.

(In biblical usage the terms "evil spirit" or "unclean spirit" or "demon" refer to the same thing. Because of phobias and ridiculous images conjured up in our minds around the word "demon" and because the term communicates better the insights I'm seeking to share, I prefer the designation "evil spirit.")

As the New Testament tells it, evil spirits are involved in violence (Matt. 8:28), muteness (Matt. 9:32), blindness (Matt. 12:22), personal suffering (Matt. 15:22), epilepsy (Matt. 17:15), anti-social behavior, incorrigibility, and self-punishment (Mark 5:2–5), harrassment (Luke 6:18–19), loneliness and isolation (Luke 8:29), screaming (Luke 9:39), physical deformity (Luke 13:11, 16), betrayal (Luke 22:3), inner torment (Acts 5:16), and clairvoyance (Acts 16:16).

Not every sickness is said to be caused by an evil spirit. But some are. Not every emotional/spiritual disorder is said to be the activity of a devil. But some are clearly said to result from control or harrassment by evil spirits.

The believer's normal response to sin is to acknowledge it, recognize its destructiveness, accept God's forgiveness for it, and change (repent). This is always the place to begin. But some long-standing emotional reaction-patterns are set so deeply as to be, apparently, beyond personal power to choose. If this is true, could such a problem-area be the scene of struggle against an inner evil spirit? Could an unholy personage have taken advantage of early ignorance, fear, and the like to assume control over some facet of the person's subconscious life?

I doubt that merely shouting "Demon begone!" will solve the spirit-problems of most people.[8] I think there are multitudes bound by evil spirits who cannot be unchained without extensive sacrifice on the part of someone spiritually sensitive and willing enough to pay the price of continuing servanthood demanded for the brother's deliverance. ("This kind can come out only by prayer and fasting!" Mark 9:29, margin.)

Ultimately, Jesus' grace must be applied to the diseased area. But never hurriedly. It may be necessary to return to it again and again, to be certain the inner pain is fully dealt with and that the cleansed house isn't opened again to the same destructive spirit (Matt. 12:43–45). If not thoroughly felt, faced, expressed, confronted, expelled, and cleansed by the Holy Spirit, there is danger that a bitter spirit may merely go into hiding, covered again, this time with a theological or psychological sugar coating. For this reason there must be full, continuing inner disclosure of the truth (reality); full, continuing agreement with God about any sin involved; full, continuing appropriation of God's forgiveness, acceptance, and cleansing; full, continuing surrender to the inner workings of the Holy Spirit; and full, continuing responsiveness to the voice and Word of God.

In the light of Scripture I delight to describe the process as I have. Psychologists and primal therapists will doubtless describe it from their perspective and in very different terms. The evil spirits they seek, by their chosen psychological methodologies, to exorcize, have all been given scientific names which describe destructive effects in the lives of the victims. While largely rejecting the idea of demons as unscientific and superstitious, they nonetheless are engaged in a ministry of deliverance, with varying degrees of success. The degree of success, I suppose, is related to the degree of purposeful or unconscious alignment with God's healing principles which they and their patients achieve.[9]

Jesus specifically makes curing folks from the effects of evil spirits part of the church's healing commission (Luke 9:1-2 and Mark 16:17). Is there not something here for the church to re-research, rethink, and re-apply? There is much we do not understand about emotional/spiritual illnesses and destructive personality defects, their causes and cures. At the same time, ironically, there exists a dearth of understanding about evil spirits and the biblical ministry of deliverance. Yet both the Lord and the early church saw such a ministry as a vital part of their healing task. And our generation overflows with needy people—even in the church—who await such a ministry. Is it conceivable that this vacuum of understanding might be filled and the unmet needs of many people in the church might be served by the development and application of a new "theology of inner healing" which harmonizes biblical teaching and Jesus' ministry of deliverance with the true truth in psychology?

To Be Pure in Heart

Six weeks after an initial forty hours of therapy, while on a teaching assignment in Hawaii, I had a priceless spiritual experience. There had been a few serious "downs" since my days in "the PIT." Though painful, they were short-lived and I seemed to have a whole new set of "handles" for dealing constructively with them. For the most part, I was feeling better about myself and what was happening in my life than I had for years. The following journal entry illustrates what was beginning to happen . . .

> The three-hour time difference between Phoenix and Kona has created havoc with my sleep. I was wide awake this morning at three.
> "Surely," thought I, "I'll soon go back to sleep for another three or four hours."

The Incredible Hope

I decided to spend the time meditating. Going through my head was an idea (not a quote) from Psalm 119 which I had read to Audrey a couple of nights ago.

> I will meditate on Thy precepts in the night watches.

"Which of God's precepts shall I meditate on?" said one side of my mind to the other side of my mind.

"I don't know."

"I'll ask God to tell me what to think about." So I did.

A couple of commandments slipped in and then out of my thought channel—I can't recall which ones. Then followed a couple of verses from somewhere in the Bible. But my meditation-ready mind failed to latch on to any of these.

Then clear as crystal came the words,

> Blessed are the pure in heart.[10]

"Now there's something to think about!" said one side of my mind to the other.

My meditation on this precept went something like this (with a lot more repetition and mulling over each idea):

"Pure in heart" ... That means "single" ... single-minded. ... To focus exclusively on God ... No adulterations or secondary motivations or complex rationalizations ... Simply and completely taken with God and Jesus and the Holy Spirit ... Completely fixed, fully concentrated on His ways and His reality ... No distractions ...

> Cleanse your hands you sinners, purify your hearts you double-minded: weep and wail, turn your joy into mourning and your laughter into crying. Humble yourself before God and He will lift you up.

(It was an inaccurate quotation of James 4:8-10. But no matter—the Lord, speaking over the faulty circuits of my limited human brain, nonetheless gets His message through.)

"It's the process I've been going through," I mused. It's what Primal Therapy has been for me: Cleansing my hands ... purifying my heart ... making my mind single instead of confusedly double ... weeping and wailing over sin and because of sin ... crying ... humbling myself.

I became consciously excited as I realized that God, faithful to His Word, has been taking me toward singleness of mind (intellect, feelings, and will all saying the same thing). The potential of becoming pure in heart (emotions, will) suddenly flashed as a bright, real hope.

"On with it, Lord!" I said aloud. "I *really* want it. To be all for You, engulfed in You, the entire thrust of my inner and outer life concentrated toward You.

"But how will it be expressed?"

The answer was right there in my mouth the instant I asked.

> Thou shalt love the Love thy God
> with all thy heart
> with all thy soul
> with all thy mind
> with all thy strength.[11]

That is to be pure in heart. That is what the pure in heart are doing every moment of every day.

"Let me love You like that, Lord. I feel that everything I've been through these past two years—all the heart-searching and painful dealing with my internal emotional blockages—has been so that I could (at last) be free to love You.

"I *want* to love You. I *choose* to love You . . .

with all my heart

—every emotion loving You. I understand my emotions better now. I have more control over them. I'm more prepared than ever to turn all my emotional energy—by my new freedom of choice—to the happy task of loving You . . .

with all my soul

—every facet of my psyche, my personality, loving You. My psyche has been so twisted and sick for so long (all its disease is still not completely healed). But enough healing has come so that vast areas of my personality are now reachable. With new knowledge and new light and new influence over who I am, I am ready to discover what it means to give my whole personality, all that I am psychologically, to the work of loving You . . .

with all my mind

—my intellect and reason, my capacity to know and think,

concentrating on loving You. Free from confusion from dissident subconscious voices, guilts, and double motives, I am becoming able to throw my entire intellectual life into my relationship with You, loving You . . .

with all my strength
—every function of my body, all my physical energies and urges, whatever I am doing can now be engaged in loving You. Energy, once diverted to fear and defensive hostilities, may now be used to demonstrate the reality of my love for You."

At that moment, my arms were raised skyward. Through happy tears I praised and thanked my God for bringing me to this place in my life. The struggle seemed worth it. I welcomed His fresh invasion of everything I am. I made new surrenders and expressed new desires to be completely His. I loved Him and told Him I wanted to love Him as perfectly as He wants to be loved. We loved each other.

I thought I might burst with the joy. The Sun was rising on a brand-new day!

——— • ———

Let every minute today be a minute to love You, Father. Today, I want to be one of the pure in heart.

CHAPTER 10

Strength Is Perfected in Weakness

To keep me from becoming conceited because of these surpassingly great revelations, there was given me a thorn in my flesh, a messenger of Satan, to torment me. Three times I pleaded with the Lord to take it away from me. But he said to me, "My grace is sufficient for you, for my power is made perfect in weakness." Therefore, I will boast all the more gladly about my weaknesses, so that Christ's power may rest on me. That is why, for Christ's sake, I delight in weaknesses, in insults, in hardships, in persecutions, in difficulties. For when I am weak, then I am strong (2 Cor. 12:7–10).

If ever a statement had the mocking ring of sheer nonsense, it is Paul's in Second Corinthians 12:9—"Power is made perfect in weakness."

To add to the assault on intelligence, he claims God personally spoke these self-contradictory words to him. And further, he dares to rest the whole case for the validity of his apostolic ministry on such foolishness as this!

I find myself irresistably attracted to this bizarre proposition because at no other time in my life have I felt so weak, so at the mercy of my inadequacies, so tattered with spiritual discrepancies. As never before, my weakness and neediness stand exposed to those who know me. My children know their daddy is "in therapy" for his unresolved emotional conflicts. My church family knows, my pastoral colleagues know, the specific problem areas being dealt with. It is a bit hard to maintain an image of strength when those with whom one is supposed to minister are quite aware that one's spiritual sickness is so serious that "professional help" must be sought.

> My kids just left for church. Without me. I have been instructed to stay out of situations in which I am expected to, and easily do, fall into the old "leadership role." It is a temporary course I am to take during the period of intensive therapy, to free me from pressures that push me back into destructive patterns of response in which I function from a highly guilt-motivated sense of responsibility. It is hoped that in the process new patterns, more in keeping with freedom and faith, can be developed.
> The intensity of guilt and shame I feel at this moment makes this a most difficult instruction to follow. I am trembling inside with fear of what the people of the church—and my kids—must be thinking of me. I am certain they feel I am "letting them down." Inside, condemning voices and long, accusing fingers declare without question: "You *are* letting them down!"
> When they arrive at the meeting, my children will have to answer the embarrassing questions: "Where's Dad?" "How is your father doing?" And the implied question, "Why didn't your dad come with you?"
> Self-loathing boils up from the secret slime-pit inside me at the thought of a father (me) who would put his kids through such a difficult ordeal. I want to go to my bed and cover up my head with a blanket and never show my face again—to my kids or the church.
> "God's man of faith and power" has admitted before everyone important to him that he is the weakest of all! Of what use to church and family is a man as shamefully inadequate as I. "God's man of fear and failure!"—that's who I *really* am.
> I despair of ever regaining my "lost strength." Wouldn't it have been better to have continued the facade? Even as I ask myself such a question, I know instinctively that there is *no more energy available for pulling off the deception.* Em-

barrassing as it is, I must now be what I am, and my peers must know.

For a long time I have felt life was getting out of my hands. When I was younger, my defense mechanisms worked well and I could evade the issue of my spiritual crippledness. My life was fairly well controlled, and I was able to function in my various roles with apparent confidence, in spite of the unresolved internal problems. Apparently, only my marriage relationship suffered the direct destructive force of the undealt-with secret confiicts. But turning forty-three was like flipping a switch in my inner life (others are hit by this at 30, 40, or 50, but for me it was 43!). The defenses that had served me so well began to give way. The "secret" issues began to cry out for resolution. Unfulfilled biblical promises of wholeness began to haunt the realities of my life. I experienced increasing difficulty in "playing the game" of adequacy and fulfillment. The healing principles of self-disclosure (1 John 1) and of truth-in-the-inward-parts (Ps. 51:6) became more important than maintaining an image of strength.

I am a tired old fan dancer whose arthritic fingers keep dropping the tattered, flimsy fans she's been using to cover her aging nakedness. One by one the dubious coverings are falling away, until I stand exposed for all who care (or dare) to look and see.

And I see myself.

I am so ashamed, so bitterly grief-struck to discover that, while others are strong, *I* am weakness personified.

Power, Perfection, and Weakness

Paul was always in trouble with some people in the church at Corinth who could not accept him as a bonafide apostle because he was so uncharismatic. They could see glaring weakness in the man. And he resolutely refused to look, speak, or act like a superstar.

His response to their criticism is startling: "It is my weaknesses—so obvious and irritating to you all—which actually gave the power of God a chance to do its work!"

It was, as I've already pointed out, God Himself who put

such a strange idea into Paul's head. It shatters many of Christendom's treasured illusions. Contrary to popular opinion among the saints, God is not interested in producing self-contained spiritual giants who appear powerful and are recognized by the world as powerful. He seeks human vessels through whom to demonstrate His own power in ways which convince observers that the power is God's. The weakness of the weak provided exactly the setting He desired for revealing His strength, for the simple reason that the weak (whose weaknesses are known) can never get away with taking the credit.

The original word for power, here in Second Corinthians 12:9, is *dunamis*. English derivatives include dynamite, dynamo, and dynamic. The following statement of principle places several of the concepts contained in the term *dunamis* in the Second Corinthians 12:9 perspective:

> Power, strength, ability, energy, effectiveness, might, authority, and majesty are perfected in weakness.[1]

The original word translated "perfect" is *teleos*: i.e., finished, completed, concluded, fulfilled, carried out into full operation, realized.[2] According to the Second Corinthians 12:9 principle, weakness is the catalyst or environment which serves to allow God's power to reach its zenith of effectiveness.

The word for weakness is *astheneia*. It covers most of the ideas normally attached to the word *weakness*: i.e., want of strength, feebleness, bodily infirmity, a state of ill health, sickness, frailty, imperfections, suffering, affliction, distress, and calamity.[3] Not just "natural human weakness" as a general category in contrast to "supernatural divine power," but every specific kind of weakness or difficulty experienced by people in the course of their lives. And each is something which, in believers, can be used to perfect the power of God.

Amazing!

God lacks nothing, needs no one and is, in Himself, absolute, self-existent and fully sovereign over everything in the created universe. *God's power is perfect and fully able to accomplish anything the will of God elects to accomplish.* There will always be more energy available in God than our deepest need can exhaust or our wildest imaginings can fathom (Eph. 3:20). But His astounding secret, whispered to Paul, is that there is a sense (established by His own Grand Design) in which God's power is imperfect, incomplete, and unable to operate at full effectiveness . . . except in the presence of weakness. The infiniteness and limitlessness of God's strength remains untapped, unknown, and unexperienced, until a situation is provided in which there are acknowledged needs which the divine *dunamis* may serve. Every imaginable human weakness or difficulty provides God's power with such a setting for demonstration.

Gallery of Powerlessness

As he leads to this fantastic statement of principle—"strength is perfected in weakness"—Paul tells of his own weaknesses. This section (2 Cor. 11-12) has been called "Paul's defense of his apostleship." He insists, to the contrary, that it is not a defense at all, but something he is saying "in Christ . . . for your strengthening" (12:19). He shares out of concern that believers grow up and become *truly* strong.

Here is one of the strangest descriptions of a "spiritual giant" ever recorded:

He is not a skillful speaker (11:6). This either means he is not an eloquent orator, or that he had some kind of speech impediment. He details it further in an earlier letter (1 Cor. 2:1-5).

He has a tendency to be in bondage to those who are paying his support. He speaks of his refusal to accept financial help from the Corinthians while ministering among them (11:7-9). Reasons given are to "elevate" those to whom he is ministering (v. 7), and to keep "from being a burden to you in any way" (v. 9). He wanted them to have no question that his concern was for them, not for the living he could make from them. But in his first letter he hints at a more basic personal motive behind his refusal of support: That he might be "free and belong to no man" (1 Cor. 9:19).

Could it have been that Paul feared that acceptance of material support would place on him a sense of obligation to please his contributors, which might cause him to "pull his punches"?

Was he afraid he might be tempted to "play to the gallery," or to minister from a position of bondage to other voices, rather than have freedom to obey only the voice of God?

He was a "weak leader" (2 Cor. 11:21)—at least compared to some of the other teachers and leaders gaining a following in the church. He does not for a minute believe it is true. He knows his strength as a spiritual helmsman. But there are Christians who think a good leader is one who "carries himself" like a leader, speaks like a leader, makes heavy demands on people, and uses them to further his own ministry. This is the kind of leader many people are looking for and will follow.

By these standards Paul's leadership is weak. He doesn't pull rank, throw his weight around, or take away anyone's freedom in the course of his leadership. He places a high value on the sovereignty of those he seeks to lead. And those who are measuring by the world's standard of measure misunderstand that kind of servant-leadership and call it "weakness."

Then, beginning in verse 23, his list of frailties, infirmities, and failures grows quickly:

> He works harder than other Christian leaders, making his own way (v. 23)
>
> He has been in prison more (v. 23)
>
> He has been beaten more times (he can't remember how often, NASB) (v. 23)
>
> Five times he has received the infamous "thirty-nine lashes" from his own countrymen, the Jews (v. 24)
>
> Three times he has been beaten with clubs (v. 25)
>
> He has suffered the humiliation and agony of public stoning (v. 25)
>
> Three times ships he was sailing on were destroyed in the sea (v. 25)
>
> He is almost never home (v. 26)
>
> He has been in danger from the elements (v. 26)
>
> He has been in danger from bandits (v. 26)
>
> His own countrymen hate him (v. 26)—they consider him a traitor (Acts 21:27–36)
>
> The Gentiles hate him (v. 26)
>
> Even church people ("false brothers") hate him and work to undercut his ministry (v. 26)

Strength Is Perfected in Weakness 141

He has been in trouble in every place you can name: in the city, in the desert, in the sea (v. 26).

Does this sound like the "triumphal procession" we thought he was describing in Second Corinthians 2:14? And there is more in verse 27:

Hard work
Hardship
Sleepless nights
Hunger ("often without food")
Thirst
Cold
Not enough clothing to keep warm.

And that is merely the "external" history of his struggle. In verses 28 and 29 he confesses personal weakness in that he continually feels the pressure of concern for all the churches. Whenever anyone in the churches is weak or failing or suffering, this sensitive man of God *feels* it. The strong seem to trust God with every problem and go on about their work. But when anyone in the churches stumbles into sin, Paul feels the fire of intense concern ("I burn for them!"). A strong leader would keep things in better balance, and not die with every sinner and suffer with every spiritual lapse. But this man hurts when saints stumble.

Then, as if propelled by an obsession, the apostle proceeds to spill forth still more . . .

"In Damascus, I achieved such city-wide acclaim for my preaching in the centers of power, that the king decided to arrest me. I barely escaped (see 11:32–33).

"And I have more weaknesses of which to boast: I have a problem tendency to exalt myself for past spiritual experiences. This pride is such a problem that God has had to deal with it constantly, through an embarrassing physical weakness He refuses to take away" (see 12:7).

Before chapter 12 ends, he has added to his infamous list:

Unanswered prayer (v. 8–9)
Insults (v. 10)
Distresses (v. 10)
Persecutions (v. 10)
Difficulties (v. 10)

Fear of disappointment (v. 20)
Fear of rejection (v. 20)
Fear of facing difficult situations (v. 20)
Fear that God will humiliate him by allowing him to show weakness in front of the very people who are looking for weaknesses as an excuse for rejecting him (v. 21)
Fear that he will break down and cry publicly (v. 21)
Fear that they will not listen to him, but will persist in their sinful ways (v. 21).

I have felt the embarrassment, the humiliation, the stinging sense of defeat, the weight of the shepherd's burden, the fear. I have escaped most of the physical suffering Paul speaks of, and have experienced only a little trouble from secular enemies, but I identify profoundly with the distress, the heavy load, the burning, and the sense of powerlessness.

How many of these things are useable for displaying the power of God?

All! Our visible weakness is important to the perfection of power.

Power Minus Weakness Equals Trouble

A focus on glorious spiritual experiences, power, and success, without transparency regarding weakness, leads to spiritual problems, says Paul in Second Corinthians 12:1–7. He would love to be telling about an out-of-this-world experience of fourteen years ago. He saw visions of Paradise (v. 4) and received spectacular revelations from the Lord Himself (Gal. 1:12, 16). Were he to tell these powerful, positive things, it is even possible the skeptical Corinthians might be more inclined to accredit his apostleship. But that was fourteen years ago. And the power of Christian leadership lies not in past experiences alone. A person must have a history with God, but power is more than a memory of power. What is needed is present energy for today's realities.

There are at least two dangers in telling only power stories:

1. Without the disclosure of true weakness, it is possible for people to be mislead in their evaluation of God's servant.

> I refrain [from boasting of glowing past experiences],
> so no one will think more of me than is warranted by
> what I do or say (1 Cor. 12:6, brackets added).

It is important that people of God be known for who they are, and what they are experiencing at the present time. The chief function of servant-leaders is to model for the church what it means to walk with God in every kind of circumstance. This requires a life purposely lived in a "glass house" as a "visible Christian."

God's power is not demonstrated, primarily, in grand and ecstatic experiences. He demonstrates His power in weaknesses and failures.

2. Without the disclosure of true weakness, God's servant may forget who he really is and fall into the trap of self-exaltation (v. 7). If one shares only "the good stuff" of his Christian life (even though it is true), before long he ceases to be exalting God with his testimony, and has begun exalting himself. He always looks good, faithful, adequate, obedient, victorious, heroic, even though the realities of his life are the same as everyone else's—a mixture of joy and pain, faith and doubt, grace and weakness, walking and stumbling, and so on. Sharing it all is what allows the glory of God to come through. God's power is not, to any degree, limited or diminished by our telling the whole truth, positive and negative, about our lives in Christ.

The Thorn

Conditioned as I am to the way church leaders (including myself) usually function, I certainly never expected to hear "the great apostle of the church" express himself with the kind of candor he manifests in telling about his "thorn."

> I experienced these tremendous visionary flights into Paradise. I saw things that the limiting laws of human speech make impossible to tell. Wow! would I love to tell that story again. These experiences were powerful and real. They changed my life.
> But let me tell you a more recent experience that is even more powerful.
> Because my early experiences with Christ were so

"super-great" and because I have a troublesome tendency to become conceited about them, God has given me a special unwanted gift to keep my pride in balance. He has given me a "thorn in my flesh." Actually, it is the kind of thing that is so tormenting it could only be the work of the devil himself. But God permits the enemy to afflict me in this way to keep me from exalting myself (12:1–7, paraphrased).

What was this thorny messenger from Satan? Various Bible scholars think the things Paul writes about himself in his letters suggest several possibilities, i.e., bad eyes or a speech impediment or epilepsy or a bad marriage, and so on. We know from his letters that he was intense. Could he have been such an intense personality that his intensity hindered his relationships with people? He was repeatedly rejected. He may have been the kind of person who really hurts when others do not accept him. Could super-sensitivity have been the nagging, deflating thorn?

Paul purposely did not specify the exact nature of the thorn so that each of us would be left to think it might have been the same as our own, and could apply his message immediately to ourselves.

He hates the presence of this diabolical infirmity. So he prays repeatedly for deliverance from its embarrassing presence. The Heavenly Father's persistent answer is "No."

> My grace is sufficient for you, for my power is made perfect in weakness.

The revelation of the thorn is: *When we are strong in our own eyes, God must, in His lovingkindness, bring us to weakness, so that we can discover His strength.*

At Peace With What I Am

When one grasps the truth that his weaknesses are the launching pad for the power of God, his whole attitude toward himself may change . . .

> I am *well content* with weaknesses (12:10 NASB, italics added).

Contentment. How my insides have ached for it!

I have spent much of my life's energy trying to keep my faults and frailties from surfacing—terrified of being found out for the weakling I am. I have been like a man in a swimming pool desperately struggling to keep a score of beach balls submerged, by keeping them under his body. He has time or energy for little else. When he decides to stop the ridiculous struggle and allows the balls to pop up to the surface, he can relax and enjoy his swim.

When I let my weaknesses be known—give up my desperate fight to appear strong—it is a great relief. A kind of peace comes in simply giving up the buffoonish battle of the buried beach balls. I begin to relax with being who I am. I can even find joy in my weaknesses.

... At least that's Paul's experience. He advances beyond mere acknowledgment of his inadequacies to: Delight (NIV); Enjoyment (Phillips); Pleasure (Amplified); Contentment (NASB); in his frailties and struggles.

Has his fragile mind finally snapped? No.

He finds contentment in his weaknesses because: 1) he sees them not as enemies, but (by grace) he has broken through to the insight that they are in his life "for Christ's sake" (v. 10) and; 2) the revelation is grasped (by faith) that "When I am weak, then I am strong" (v. 10).

Good news for strugglers: *It is all right to feel good about who you are and what you are like . . . including your weaknesses.*

Weakness on Mission

It may seem foolish to some who still believe God can use only the strong or the perfect—and, because I am so weak and failing, I may often look and feel like a spiritual nobody—but the truth is that God is at work in my life. I am "on mission" for Him. Weakness does not disqualify me for service. On the contrary: "Power is perfected in weakness."

Even the power of an apostle (2 Cor. 12:11–12).

Out of the Struggle, A Song

At a time when I felt the most ineffective and fraught with "thorns," *Decision* magazine carried the story of the Christian poet, William Cowper (pronounced Cooper). This article and some of Cowper's hymns have become a source of courage for me. For I identify deeply with this sensitive, emotionally unstable Englishman of the late 1700s.

Cowper lost his mother when he was a boy. He lived for ten years in a succession of homes and institutions. He was denied the woman he loved and wished to marry. Within a few months of this heartbreak, his father, whom he also loved, died of a stroke. Within days of the death of his father, his best friend was drowned. Cowper had always been highly sensitive, shy, and introspective. Now, in his loneliness and grief, he became deeply depressed and consumed with self-pity.

After failing to win a coveted post in the House of Lords—because of his intense shyness and fear—in the winter of 1763, William Cowper suffered a mental breakdown.

> Melancholia took on the form of vicious headaches, terrifying dreams, and unreasoning paranoia. He could not sleep. He hated life and attempted suicide three times.
>
> ... It was during these days of mental torment that Cowper first heard the message of forgiveness found in Jesus Christ. At first he was too absorbed in his own pain to comprehend that the gift was for him. A few months later, however, while convalescing at the private asylum of a dedicated Christian, truth at last came into Cowper's distorted reason. He was reading Romans 3:25: "Whom God hath set forth to be a propitiation through faith in his blood, to declare his righteousness for the remission of sins that are past, through the forebearance of God" (KJV). New hope filled the broken poet.[4]

Cowper was no longer alone. God became his companion and comfort. Christians accepted him warmly. A believing family and church took him in and provided security and confidence he had never known before. His literary gift, ignited by the Holy Spirit, now proclaimed the Good News.

> And yet, for the rest of his life, Cowper continued to be beset by attacks of recurring melancholia, sometimes distorting his perceptions and robbing him of hope and confidence.
>
> Cowper never fully overcame these emotional struggles in his life. But his victory came through quiet confidence, day after day:

> "Tis my happiness below,
>   Not to live without the cross,
> But the Savior's power to know,
>   Sanctifying every loss:
> Trials must and will befall;
>   But with humble faith to see
> Love inscribed upon them all,
>   This is happiness to me."[5]

As I have struggled against my own brand of "melancholia," with its attending sense of shame and failure, I have become painfully aware that I am involved in a continuing battle by faith against sin and its effects in my life. When I heard of William Cowper's struggles, and saw that there had been a man of God as weak as I whom God had used, I began to search my hymnals for his poetry. Remembering that God was with him and how, in the same way, He is with me in my weakness, I began to sing with new understanding and hopeful appropriation a Cowper hymn I first heard while still a baby, sitting on my mother's lap in church:

> There is a fountain filled with blood
>   Drawn from Immanuel's veins;
> And sinners, plunged beneath that flood,
>   Lose all their guilty stains.
>
> The dying thief rejoiced to see
>   That fountain in his day;
> And there may I, though vile as he,
>   Wash all my sins away.
>
> Thou dying Lamb, thy precious blood
>   Shall never lose its power,
> Till all the ransomed Church of God
>   Be saved, to sin no more.
>
> E'er since, by faith, I saw the stream
>   Thy flowing wounds supply,
> Redeeming love has been my theme,
>   And shall be till I die.
>
> Then in a nobler, sweeter song,
>   I'll sing thy power to save,
> When this poor lisping, stammering tongue
>   Lies silent in the grave.[6]

In God's topsy-turvy approach to power He takes weak, scarred, scared, struggling, failing, and ineffective people and accomplishes His mighty work with such miserably inadequate tools. In God's foolish design, He can only fulfill His goals in the visibly, admittedly weak.

> God chose the foolish things of the world to shame the wise; God chose the weak things of the world to shame the strong. He chose the lowly things of this world and the despised things—and the things that are not—to nullify the things that are, so that no one may boast before him. It is because of him that you are in Christ Jesus, who has become for us wisdom from God—that is, our righteousness, holiness and redemption. Therefore, as it is written: "Let him who boasts boast in the Lord" (1 Cor. 1:27–31).

CHAPTER 11

The Creator's Non-Verbal Communication

And God saw all that He had made, and behold, it was very good (Gen. 1:31 NASB).

A Walk in the Rain

It stormed Friday night, about eleven o'clock. I stood at the window and blinked at blinding flashes of summer lightning, and felt-as-much-as-heard the explosive crash of nearby thunder. Torrents of rainwater washing down roofs, porches, and walks sounded angry. I watched turmoiled sheets of rain swirl across the pavement under the streetlight, and I identified with the turmoil. It suited my mood completely. I was angry, guilty, depressed, and it was all intensified by a sense of helplessness. But the storm seemed to me to be saying it felt some of these things too.

After a while, with the storm beginning to subside, I went to bed. Audrey and I prayed before going to sleep. Mine was a prayer which reflected the storm of fear and frustration inside.

My depression persisted through Saturday. I talked with a Christian friend about my feelings.

On Sunday morning, the monsoons returned, more gently this time.

About eight o'clock, Audrey was standing by the open window. "It's an 'Oregon' rain," she said.

I was still in bed, intending to "sleep in." But with my face in the pillow, I mumbled, half-joking, "Let's go for a walk."

"Do you want to?"

I sat up on the edge of the bed. "Let's do it!"

Quickly—for such rains come and go quickly in the desert—we dressed. Well . . . not completely. I went shirtless in a pair of walking shorts. Audrey wore only shorts and a light top. Barefoot and hatless, two forty-seven-year olds, uncertain if they really ought to be doing such a childish thing, sallied forth into the rain.

The gentle rain felt cool and exhilarating on bare skin. A sensation which, for too many years, we'd hurried under shelter to escape.

We walked around our long city block holding hands, laughing at our selves. We were sure the neighbors had more reason than ever to know that we are crazy. We splashed in overflowing gutters, walked on wet grass, squished what mud we could find (that had not been asphalted or concreted) between our toes.

About halfway 'round the block, our "Oregon" rain turned into a subtropical cloudburst. It was glorious! To walk and to get soaked to the skin and to delight in the whole silly process!

When we returned home, our clothes needed to be wrung out and our hair had to be toweled dry and our neighbors had something to talk about. But our spirits were lifted. We felt cleansed in body, mind, and spirit. And we were praising God.

And we were wondering why, for all these years of trying so hard to do God's work, we had not taken time *every* time it rained to put off our shoes and our dignity and be the kids we really are longing inside to be.

I reflected on all the stuffy, meaningless, church business meetings whose dreary agenda might have been given a new lease on life, had we dared to take a break and dance in the rain that fell outside. I thought about sermons which might have been refreshed and made alive, had I interrupted my arduous study to take off my shirt and join in the watery revival God was sending outside.

I began to sense that, in the search for giftedness, there is something extremely important about coming into full touch with the Creator's world. For, with all that God has created me to be—my special gifts, my uniqueness from other parts of creation, my Spirit-led want-to's and even my limitations—I am part of the whole great creative work He has done.

Could it be that I do not know who I am and where I fit and what I should be doing, simply because I am disconnected from the rest of creation? Could it be that I have not paid enough attention to His voice speaking in the natural universe (Ps. 19:1-6), and instead, have been diverted by influences which have got me going in dissidence to, and not in harmony with, His creation? I am His creation too. He has made me what I am. In new creation He is restoring what was lost in the Fall. To know what I am created to be—His original, authentic design for me—do I not need to tune in more sharply on the sensitivities and yearnings and natural characteristics He has created in me?

Is it not most likely that His Word, His special will, His good pleasure for me, will be found to be in full symphony with my createdness?

As I thought about the feeling of walking half-naked in the rain with woman by my side, it seemed as though I had come into a freshened sense of my oneness with the universe. At least, it raised the possibility in my mind that comprehension of my relationship with grass and trees and mud and rain and clouds and sky and persons is as necessary to discovery of, and contentment with, my giftedness and of where I belong in His plan, as is searching the Scriptures and praying about it. If my emaciated childish enjoyment of God's created world could be restored to full health, perhaps I could find freedom to enjoy who and what I am, and have the time of my life doing what I want to do that God wants me to do!

Enjoying the Simple Pleasures

A spiritual growth inventory uncovered in me, among other weaknesses, tendencies toward perfectionism and toward compulsiveness.

Perfectionism is . . .

> a futile and energetic effort to do things "perfectly."
> Some things need to be done that way if possible. A

column of figures should not be added up carelessly, nor do we want a surgeon to operate on us haphazardly. But "perfectionism" is a too-rigid, fear-ridden effort to "be perfect," or to do some things perfectly which do not really require that kind of tortured effort . . . This may range all the way from harmless picture straightening to . . . fear of criticism if you do something less than perfectly. This trait can result from rigidity, and makes for undue tension and anxiety. (From a Yokefellow slip, with my name at the top.[1])

Compulsiveness . . .

Your excessive tendency toward compulsiveness is adding to the strain of life, and you may have developed a few phobias (fears). This stems from anxiety, worry and a general lack of confidence. In an effort to relieve anxiety, you may have become overly cautious . . . Probably you feel anxious and guilty if things are not done in a certain way. You may have hostile feelings which you reject because you feel guilty about them, and this causes your anxiety. By learning to admit and accept these feelings . . . the need for compulsiveness will disappear as anxiety lessens. (From a Yokefellow slip, with my name at the top.[2])

Compulsiveness is expressed in my personality in the way I eat, work, and tear my fingers, among other things.

The assignment for dealing with these rigid, anxious traits of mine, which seemed to me a strange response, was to "read Genesis, chapters 1–2, and see how the plan of God for Adam involved enjoyment of the simple pleasures. God does not mean for us to feel guilty and anxious, but to enjoy life . . . Each day practice the art of relaxing and turning your 'unacceptable' feelings over to God. He understands, and forgives, and has promised:

I came that you might have life, and have it abundantly (John 10:10)."

Evidently, perfectionism and compulsiveness are linked to "uptightness" and worldly pressures and even to civilization itself.

Genesis 1 and 2 tell the sweet and simple story of the goodness and integrity of the natural world. All physical things—minerals, land, sea, sky, stars, vegetation, fish, birds, land animals, and even man—are gifts of God. All are lovely things God has done. All are things God sees as good.

As I read, I felt a deep yearning to be more in touch with the natural world. Guilt and tension, anxiety and phobias, all came after the first two chapters of Genesis. And even now, man (me), hassled as he is by the results of sin with its wrenching of relationships, may still touch the simplicity and God-relatedness of those early days, by looking at the things God was looking at and seeing them as God sees them—good.

Everyone knows that relationships are more complex than that. Going out to see a cactus bloom or a river run is not the solution to one's need for nearness to God or wife or anyone else. But there is something of God out there—something of God we can see, touch, smell, hear, taste, and breathe—in simple natural wonders which, even though our sin makes them groan (Rom. 8:22), nonetheless are the visible fingerprints of the Living God.

God has given all this natural goodness to us. Thoughtlessly, we wall ourselves in away from it, cover it up with asphalt and concrete, and drown out its music with electronically amplified noise. But when I take myself out of this man-made prison of purported progress, even in my imagination, I can get a sense of the goodness and splendor of God.

Here is an astounding discovery: Even *I* have splendor. I too am from God. He gave special attention to creating me. He made me for His enjoyment and then gave to me, for my enjoyment and to tell me about Himself, all of creation.

From what source can I get the necessary motivation to, with greater frequency, lay aside my compulsive, perfectionist over-productivity to take the time to delight in the good God has given:

In the surrounding natural scene
In my family, my wife, my daughters, my son

In friends and kin, both spiritual and natural
In my own body with its five hungry senses
In my capacity to laugh and play and relax and breathe and notice the goodness of the things God sees

Could there be something wrong with a life-consuming passion which demands that, in order to justify one's existence on this planet, one must have something of significance, something of estimable value—some work for God!—to show for every waking minute? Would it *really* be lazy of me to cease my frantic, guilty productivity to go out and climb a hill or smell a rose or skip a stone on the lake or roll in the grass with a child or contemplate for five minutes the habits of a desert bug? Or would I, in fact, be putting my fingers into the fingerprints of God?

Celebrating the Temporary

A personal discovery I am just coming into is the joy and touch with real living that comes with "celebrating the temporary." Stopping to notice and drink more deeply of *now*.

The past is past. I can learn from it but I cannot relive it. The future is to be prepared for, but I cannot live there either. Today—this moment—I have.

Now is not just a tiny, pinched, confining crevice between yesterday and tomorrow. Now is life. The only bit of life I have.

Lord, I want to live open and full and awake *now*. Remind me to smell the roses in front of my house . . . now, today. Remind me to hug my kids and my wife and tell them I love them . . . today. Remind me to breathe—I mean *really* breathe . . . today.

Grace permits me to let yesterday be. Prophecy reminds me that the future is in God's hands—and that it is something He has planned well for, for me. Today, I am alive. Today I have Jesus. Today I am involved with His people—and, with all their "warts," they are a precious gift filling my life. Today, I and they are recipients of the multiplied grace and goodness and faithful working of God!

I can see this truth in Scripture (Matt. 6:19–34, for example). But a tiny book has helped me to "see" what I am saying: *Celebrate The Temporary,* by Clyde Reid.

To celebrate the temporary is to let go worrying about yesterday and tomorrow long enough to be *here, now*. It is to give your attention, your awareness, to smelling, feeling, seeing, tasting, and hearing the myriad delights around you. To live today.[3]

God's Body-Language

Since the creation of the world God's invisible qualities—his eternal power and divine nature—have been clearly seen, being understood from what has been made, so that men are without excuse (Rom. 1:20).

Go and ask the cattle,
ask the birds of the air to inform you,
or tell the creatures that crawl to teach you,
and the fishes of the sea to give you instruction.
Who cannot learn from all these
that the Lord's own hand has done this?
              (Job 12:7–9 NEB).

The heavens tell out the glory of God,
   the vault of heaven reveals his handiwork.
One day speaks to another,
night with night shares its knowledge,
   and this without speech or language
   or sound of any voice.
Their music goes out through all the earth,
their words reach to the end of the world
              (Ps. 19:1–4 NEB).

The Speaking Stars

Tired of wrestling with such questions as: What does God want me to do with my life from here on? and Where do I fit in God's scheme?, sick of the confusion and inner conflict I have experienced as I tried to rearrange the focus of my life and work, I begged God to "write it in plain English on the wall" for me to read, because none of His other forms of communication seemed to be getting through to me or bringing me peace.

Then, the other night, after Audrey and I had eaten dinner at one of Phoenix's "cowboy steak" houses and hung around for an hour or so listening to country music, we decided to drive the thirty miles through the desert to Cave

Creek and Carefree, Arizona—just for a chance to talk. The conversation was heavy with feelings growing out of my mid-life struggle to find myself.

Cave Creek is a little village with very few streetlights. And we were soon awed by how clear and bright the stars appeared, away from the glow of the big city. We stopped the car, shut off the headlights, and got out to take in the sight. Leaning against the car we watched three "falling stars" streak and burn out against the blackness above. We commented on the nearly solid glow of the Milky Way stretching from one horizon to the other. As we talked about the vast, unimaginable distances represented above us by myriad twinkling lights, a sense of wonder wrapped us both like a warm blanket.

"If God can do all that," I couldn't resist injecting my own bitterness into the near-worship that was being shared between us, "then why can't He get through to me about what I am supposed to be doing with my life?"

Almost instantly, I realized how ridiculous the question was. Even though I was having trouble reading His signals, I knew in my heart He had already provided some pretty clear messages. He is, after all, the God Who Speaks. And I knew He was speaking to me—in His Word, in many personal revelations (insights) given by the Holy Spirit, in many of the experiences and relationships of my life at the present time. I was also aware that the barriers to decoding and understanding His messages were all inside me. If my inner emotional and spiritual blinders could be removed, I would be able to see and know.

"But why does He not just cut through those barriers and communicate to me in spite of my practiced resistances? Why doesn't He ignore my blindness and deafness and invade my mind with the clear revelation of His will? Why do I have to change before He can get through to me? He certainly is big enough to do whatever must be done."

I kept looking up and felt strangely one with the stars. They are what He made them to be. I too am what the Creator made me to be. That means I have been created in His image (Gen. 1:26). I realized, at that moment, that that meant *sovereignty*. Within created limits, man was created to rule (Gen. 1:26-28), and is free to choose many things (Gen. 2:19), including whether or not he will hear and respond to the voice of God (Gen. 2:16-17; 3:1-6).

True, the sovereign God has the power to sweep aside human sovereignty and invade my mind with His will, regardless of any conscious or unconscious, unconfronted, and unhealed internal lines of resistance in my personality. The fact that He does not, as a general rule, work that way, indicates the high priority and infinite value He places on human jurisdiction. He wants me to listen to His voice and respond because, in freedom, I choose to do so. But He knows that in me are negative emotional habits and "automatic" learned responses and fears and guilts and blinding prejudices and secret hates and unbending rigidities and patterns of rationalization and unrecognized self-deceits which disrupt my freedom to hear and to choose. And He, for the sake of bringing me into spiritual reality and restoration of lost freedom and for the sake of my future capacity to respond and to grow, elects to deal in healing ways with my basic mechanisms of response.

I can be most useful to Him if I am what I was created to be—free and sovereign. And so, He most often will reveal Himself to me through a process which deals not merely with the question I am asking (i.e., What does God want me to do for Him?) but with my lost capacity to hear His still small voice and to sovereignly choose to respond.

He evaluates my authority and liberty more highly than I do. I would welcome His invasion, His suspension of my freedom, His imposing His will upon me. That would require far less of me in terms of acceptance of personal responsibility and basic personal change. But He made me to be a god. And to further His recreative work in me aimed at restoring me to His high creative purpose, He is leading me through a healing process, a sometimes painful internal metamorphosis, to renew my capacity to hear His voice and to elect to obey it in freedom.

Having been spoken to by the stars, I am waiting and cooperating with His process, in hope (Rom. 8:24-25).

CHAPTER 12

Spiritual Sickness and Its Cure

I will make up to you the years that the swarming locust has eaten, the creeping locust, the stripping locust, and the gnawing locust, My great army which I sent among you (Joel 2:25 NASB).

Death of Sovereignty

One of the most illustrious madmen of all time was Nebuchadnezzar, King of the vast Babylonian Empire, whose splendid reign was interrupted for seven years while he lived in the wild like an animal, sleeping under the stars, running about on all fours, and eating grass like a cow—completely out of touch with reality.

When his psychotic ordeal was over and reason had returned, he wrote an account of his experience in his own words for publication throughout the realm. Daniel, the prophet, includes a copy of the document among his own writings (Dan. 4). It contains revealing insights into the nature and cure of mental illness.

Nebuchadnezzar had a dream which alarmed him. Here is the story in his own words:

"Now these were the visions in my mind as I lay on my bed: I was looking, and behold, there was a tree in the midst of the earth, and its height was great. The tree grew large and became strong, and its height reached to the sky, and it was visible to the end of the whole earth. Its foliage was beautiful and its fruit abundant, and in it was food for all. The beasts of the field found shade under it, and the birds of the sky dwelt in its branches, and all living creatures fed themselves from it.

"I was looking in the visions of my mind as I lay on my bed, and behold, an angelic watcher, a holy one, descended from heaven. He shouted out and spoke as follows: 'Chop down the tree and cut off its branches, strip off its foliage and scatter its fruit; let the beasts flee from under it, and the birds from its branches. Yet leave the stump with its roots in the ground, but with a band of iron and bronze around it in the new grass of the field; and let him be drenched with the dew of heaven, and let him share with the beasts in the grass of the earth. Let His mind be changed from that of a man, and let a beast's mind be given to him, and let seven periods of time pass over him.

"This sentence is by decree of the angelic watchers, and the decision is a command of the holy ones, in order that the living may know that the Most High is ruler over the realm of mankind, and bestows it on whom He wishes, and sets over it the lowliest of men.'"[1]

The court magician-priests, master astrologers, and other advisors-to-the-king, supposedly in touch with the world of metaphysics and spirits, were summoned. But the dream's meaning stumped them all. Finally, Daniel, who had interpreted an earlier royal dream (Dan. 2), was called.

Daniel, a Hebrew, was alarmed by the insight God gave him into the dream's meaning, because it was not good news for the emperor. Nebuchadnezzar had achieved awesome greatness in the world's eyes, and in his own. But he failed to recognize his dependence on the Ultimate Sovereign who controls the distribution of power among men, "the Most High." So that he might come to this most fundamental acknowledgment, Nebuchadnezzar was warned concerning where his egotism and arrogance were taking him.

Daniel: "This is the interpretation, O King, and this is the decree of the Most High, which has come upon my lord the king: that you be driven away from mankind, and your dwelling place be with the beasts of the field, and you be given grass to eat like cattle and be drenched with the dew of heaven; and seven periods of time will pass over you, until you recognize that the Most High is ruler over the realm of mankind, and bestows it on whomever He wishes. And in that it was commanded to leave the stump with the roots of the tree, your kingdom will be assured to you after you recognize that it is Heaven that rules."[2]

His bout with insanity evidently was avertable. The dream was intended as an early warning signal. There was a way to prevent the collapse it prophesied.

Daniel further pressed the point home: "O King, may my advice be pleasing to you: break away now from your sins by doing righteousness, and from your iniquities by showing mercy to the poor, so that there may be a prolonging of your prosperity."[3]

The great royal personage ignored the mercy-filled warning. Twelve months later, his megalomania reached its zenith. Walking on the roof of the fabulous Babylonian palace he reflected in expansive allusions to what he perceived as personal invincibility and greatness: "Is this not Babylon the great, which I myself have built as a royal residence by the might of my power and for the glory of my majesty?"[4]

Before the last word of the sentence had escaped his lips a heavenly voice drowned his royal arrogance beneath the terse announcement: "King Nebuchadnezzar, to you it is declared: *sovereignty is removed from you* ... until you recognize that the Most High is ruler over the realm of mankind, and bestows it on whomever He wishes."[5]

All touch with reality left him, and immediately "His Imperial Majesty" became a snarling, loathsome animal, whom bewildered courtiers and family drove out of the palace, away from the city, where he lived like a mindless beast for seven humiliating years. He ate grass like a cow, his body was drenched with the dew, his hair grew like eagle's feathers, and his fingernails became like birds' claws.[6]

His deliverance from the disease came as dramatically as its beginning.

"At the end of that period," he writes, "I, Nebuchadnezzar, raised my eyes toward heaven, and my reason returned to me, and I blessed the Most High and praised and honored Him who lives forever. For His dominion is an everlasting dominion, and His kingdom endures from generation to generation.

And all the inhabitants of the earth are accounted as nothing, but He does according to His will in the host of heaven and among the inhabitants of earth; and no one can ward off His hand or say to Him, 'What hast Thou done?'

"At that time my reason returned to me. And my majesty and splendor were restored to me for the glory of my kingdom, and my counselors and nobles began seeking me out; so *I was reestablished in my sovereignty* and surpassing greatness was added to me.

"Now I, Nebuchadnezzar, praise, exalt and honor the King of heaven, for all His works are true and His ways just, and He is able to humble those who walk in pride."[7]

He ought to know!

Causes of Breakdown

Aside from the concept of divine decree, from the human side, Nebuchadnezzar's mental break came as a result of several factors. According to Daniel, some of them—perhaps all—were preventable.

1. The key factor was the king's failure to recognize God's ultimate sovereignty (Dan. 4:17, 25–26, 32). He did not see God as the source of his royalty, freedom, and authority. He mistakenly believed that he had made himself what he was, and that his own inherent greatness had won him his place of world leadership.

It was a serious error. God gives leadership to whomever He wishes. It is often not to great men God gives power, but "the lowliest of men" (v. 17).

No one is really free or personally sovereign who does not see himself as absolutely dependent on God and under His authority. For anyone to picture himself as free and independent without God is as preposterous as trying to picture a fish as free without water. The only independence conceivable for a creature of the sea is when it is completely engulfed in water. Without water the fish is not only helpless and floundering, it dies. Man was created for freedom, but unless he is immersed in the life-supporting depths of a living relationship with God in which God is experienced as absolutely essential to life, he can never really be free.

As Nebuchadnezzar discovered, it is madness to think one can live without submission to "the ruler of the realm of mankind."

2. The emperor's pride became delusionary (vv. 30, 37).

It is normal and healthy for a person to possess a sense of personal worth, a sound evaluation of his own abilities and accomplishments as well as his weaknesses.

> Loving yourself properly is not egotism. Egotistical people actually dislike themselves intensely. Only those who accept and like themselves are capable of true humility. Such persons tend to view themselves with amused friendly tolerance. They are not engaged in a frantic, breathless campaign to win approval and praise. Since they accept themselves, they do not need the recognition of others to bolster their sense of identity.[8]

Nebuchadnezzar, like many people in places of power or public recognition, began to "believe his own press notices." Lacking a sense of dependency on God, he began to take personal credit for *gifts*. His successes and the self-seeking cult of personality which inevitably develops around powerful people masked his human weaknesses—even from himself. Without a wholesome acknowledgment that he himself was merely a man under the authority of the Ruler-Creator, he began to see himself as master of his own destiny, answerable to no one, absolutely independent. All that his leadership accomplished, he claimed as his own—a demonstration of Nebuchadnezzar's personal power and glory (v. 30).

In spite of millions of bowing subjects, fabulous gleaming palaces, and bejeweled crowns of human accomplishment adorning his royal head, his evaluation of himself was a lie. A delusion which was prelude to his collapse.

Many a spiritual breakdown has been predetermined by a stubborn dedication to "do it *my* way." Pride is the basic sin behind all sins. It is the reason I sometimes think I have "a better idea" than God about a thousand-and-one aspects of my life. It is often the reason I cannot/will not face honestly the discrepencies between the way I respond to life and the kinds of responses called for in the teachings of Scripture. Pride is the reason many of us go unhealed, unchanged, and unrepentent in customs of life which destroy relationships, inhibit obedience, and pilfer joy.

3. Nebuchadnezzar persisted in specific kinds of sins (v. 27). He knowingly did evil when he could have chosen to do righteousness.

"I tell you the truth," said Jesus, "everyone who sins is a slave to sin" (John 8:34).

Sin, under the guise of freedom, is, in reality, a movement away from control over one's emotions, intellect, will, and life. Sin always results in loss of sovereignty (slavery). Mental illness, according to Danuel 4, is essentially loss of sovereignty. Sin and mental illness, and every emotional and spiritual defect between the two, have the same roots. Patterns of compulsive selfishness, anger, jealousy, fear, anxiety, guilt, insecurity, inferiority, and the like, are not merely personality traits to be accepted and put up with, nor are they simply "scars of the fall" to be excused—for they are clearly out of sinc with life in God's kingdom, life in the Spirit (see the Beatitudes, Matt. 5:3–10; the Sermon on the Mount, Matt. 5–7; the Love Chapter, 1 Cor. 13; for examples). Everything in our personalities which destroys relationships, ravages self-worth, and hinders the growth of true holiness, is targeted for repentance, forgiveness, cleansing—change. For such things mask, from those who are looking for reality, the developing image of Jesus.

There is no condemnation to those who are in Christ (Rom. 8:1) even when they fail to live out His full likeness. Sin cannot separate us from His grace (Rom. 8:38–39). But grace also promises a complete break-up of the old patterns of destruction (Rom. 8:2). Regardless of whose sin caused the destructive response-system to develop in us—our own or that of the authority figures in our lives or that of the culture in which we grew up—*sin is behind all spiritual and mental problems.* God fully accepts and forgives us, with all our neurotic tendencies, spiritual deficiencies, and psychological problems—but His love goes beyond acceptance and forgiveness. His predestination for us is that we shall be, in every way, whole (Rom. 8:29–30; 1 Thess. 5:23–24). Full deliverance from sin and its damage is our heritage in Jesus Christ.

4. Daniel refers to the pressure of a leadership style that

produced enemies and opposition: "If only the dream applied to those who hate you ... to your adversaries!" (Dan. 4:19 NASB).

The world's approach to leadership—achieving success (getting things done) and relating to people—often leaves the achiever isolated, lonely, under intense pressure from friends, under threat of hatred and attack by enemies, and living in fear that his weaknesses may be discovered and used against him. The Bible's approach to leadership and accomplishment is wrapped up in the concepts of personal servanthood, mercy (feeling with and involvement with people[9]), and self-giving love (Matt. 20:25–28). Daniel's corrective instructions to Nebuchadnezzar include a call to move to the servant-leader style (Dan. 4:27). A person pursuing the servant-leader style may have lonely times, be called to take many risks and be the brunt of hatred and attack, but he will also likely know intimacy, love, and support in his weaknesses.

5. The final straw that led to the break was neglect of the warnings (vv. 27–31). The signals were there of impending disaster: The dream and its interpretation; a trusted friend confronting him with the truth about himself and where his path was leading; clarification of the basic spiritual issue involved in mental soundness; a clear outline of steps to turn the course of his life around and thus avert the breakdown. And then, he was given a full year to accept the truth and begin a process of change.

Amid delusions of his own strength and invincibility, he ignored the mercy-signals. His mind snapped under the weight of his overdeveloped ego and the decree of the Lord. In utter weakness and humiliation, he lost all control over his own affairs and those of the empire.

We are not without warning signals. The Word of God, the Holy Spirit, and the state of our personal relationships confront us with the truth. The biblical precept we cannot face without rationalizing, the inner sense of dis-ease, the unhealed relationship—each may signal an area of eroding sovereignty. Consciousness of an emotional or attitudinal pattern which is destructive to relationships or one's sense of well-being is an "X" marking a spot where healing is needed.

"Break away now from your sins by doing righteousness," the prophet-statesman begged.

But Nebuchadnezzar made his choice to hurry along to his breakdown in the face of all warnings. He would not be changed unless he experienced full humiliation.

For years I thought that if I could just be free from pastoral pressures, I could bring my anger under control. Or, if I could just be forgiven one more time. Or, if my wife could change. One by one, the pressures have been removed, external changes have been arranged, many of the things I believed were "causing" the problem have been adjusted or modified or removed. But with each release of pressure, a different one came to take its place. As pastoral responsibilities decreased, guilt increased. As one tirade was forgiven, another erupted to reveal that nothing had really changed. The people around me were trying to change themselves and improve my circumstances, but the basic slavery still enchained me.

The gut-issue had to be faced. The unyielding system of fear and hostility *within me* must be dealt with. The continuing eruptions of stored-up aggression required sympathy and understanding—but those near me also needed to come to the place where they could tolerate them no longer. I must be forced by the reality God allows, to look at myself squarely and understand how critically needy I really am—or healing can never come. It will never even be sought.

My family could continue to cover for me—as they have for years. I could continue to be indulged, permitted to put on a public face of piety while continuing my destructive pattern in private. Or I could be forced by their crying "That is enough!" to face the truth and open myself to change.

So don't comfort me too much. Don't cover for me too long. Don't rationalize away my sinful emotional habits. Don't make it easy for me to avoid facing the truth about myself. Care about me. Help me to understand myself. Identify the problem. Be honest with me.

Remind me often that I am forgiven and loved by God, just the way I am. Instruct and encourage me to move toward change. Trust God for me, and help me to recognize and to believe in His working in me.

To be what God created me to be, I must be free. I must be emancipated in every area of my person in which sin now seems to reign. I will never get free without the help of people near me, who will face the truth and help me to face it too.

The Essence of Breakdown

It is obvious from what happened to Nebuchadnezzar that the human sovereignty he lost involved more than his ability to rule the kingdom. He lost the ability to control his life as a human being.

Ironically, people are given authority to make choices which take away (or give away) their freedom to choose (Gen. 3:12-13). And to compound the tragedy, one generation may, within the limits established by prevenient grace,[10] give up or undermine, to one degree or another, the sovereignty of the next generation (Exod. 20:5).

But even so, each person born into this world has important choices to make. He and the people around him have freedom to choose many things which affect his life. Every time a sinful choice is made, or a series of choices becomes a destructive behavioral pattern, potential sovereignty (freedom of choice) is lost, and replaced with a "pre-punched" program of response over which he has little or no control.

The loss of personal freedom of choice is the essence of all spiritual and emotional ill-health.

In my personality there seem to be some forces which are beyond my power to choose. When certain kinds of situations arise, without thinking (even without choosing, it seems) I react in a predetermined way, a way I am internally "programmed" to react. Certain circumstances, for instance, trigger excessive levels of fear. Yet not until I began the inward journey I've been describing in this book did I have the foggiest notion what was causing these phobias. In addition, I have excessive perfectionist tendencies, which seem to automatically control my attitudes and behavior. I also find that I am excessively dependent on others for approval and my sense of self-worth. And I have always been plagued by depression, which has often been so excessive that I could neither work nor relate to people effectively. This was so extreme that I wished to die. Often I have been unable to pinpoint the source of this depression.

In all of these cases, it has seemed to me that the choices were made somewhere in the past, at the time my "emotional computer cards" were being keypunched, and that, in the present, I can only react as I have been pre-programmed to react.

These, obviously, are my perceptions. Reality may be that I could have controlled more of my reactions than I have. But, it is also true that the tendencies and weaknesses and warps in my emotional conditioning which have led to many of these neuroses,[11] "besetting sins,"[12] and discomforting patterns of response were formed in me before I can remember (in some cases, before I was born). They are part of the legacy of sin in the family—both the family of my physical and cultural heritage (back to the third and fourth generations, Exod. 20:5) and the family of man (Rom. 5:12). To this bequeathal I have added my own sinful choices, each one in its turn putting another twist in my "second nature," setting its ruts deeper. Regardless of how I wish it were not true, I, in my turn, am passing my emotional and spiritual heritage of bondage on to my children.

The fact is, every spiritual and emotional barrier to fullness of relationship with God and each other, every fear, prejudice, or resistance blocking the way to full obedience to His will, and every mental illness or "permanent" infirmity of personality or character (regardless of who or what helped to shape it) constitutes an erosion of personal sovereignty, a loss of freedom to choose.

From Daniel 4 we may extract the principle that, when it fits His purpose, the Creator can "remove" (v. 31) His original gift of sovereignty in an affected area of human personality. The basic laws upon which the universe functions assure that sovereignty will be removed from anyone who fails to acknowledge and bow to the Lordship of God. Removal of human sovereignty does not always take the radical form it did with Nebuchadnezzar (nor is it always announced by angels) but, as Jesus said, there is no sin which is not a movement away from freedom toward enslavement (John 8:34).

Spiritual Sickness and Its Cure 169

Failure to acknowledge that "the Most High is ruler over the realm of mankind" always has disastrous results in the human personality. Rebellion against God is, in itself, a form of insanity.

God's merciful purpose in this universal system is to force the issue involved in the practice of sin, to create a yearning for the lost freedom, and to press us toward restoration and healing. (Dan. 4 is not an isolated reference to God acting out such a pattern. See also Rom. 1:24, 26, 28; 1 Cor. 5:5; Gal. 6:7–10; Heb. 12:5–11.)

The Years of the Locusts

> I will make up to you for the years
> That the swarming locust has eaten,
> The creeping locust, the stripping locust, and the gnawing locust,
> My great army which I sent among you (Joel 2:25 NASB).

In today's reading, Oswald Chambers applies this promise to things that lead sensitive people into insanity: Past things.[13]

I am thinking about my "past things." The early perception that I was not acceptable because I was a boy instead of a girl. The early taunting rejection of other children because I was "fat." My mother's death at my gateway to adolescence (when healthy independence from her would begin to be established). The misguided input of spiritual tutors who led me to believe her death could be punishment from God for childish disobedience.

I'm reflecting on the erroneous picture of God I was given . . . How it undermined spiritual stability through years of ignorance . . . And how patterns of feeling and behavior established then still infect my responses to God today.

I'm remembering my father's struggle with guilt, anger, sensitivity, and perfectionism . . . passed on to me by the combination of heredity and relational osmosis which shapes us all.

I am brooding over sinful habits I chose and unthinkingly built into myself . . . Lustful patterns of thought and response. Unholy ways of releasing tension. Deceitful, manipulative games used to get sympathy, affirmation, and love. Devious patterns of choice, blame for which can be laid at no one's feet but mine.

I am thinking about the awful reality of my great difficulty with forgiving real or supposed wrongs done to me. The self-chosen and conditioned inner hindrances to loving as Christ loves. Blockages, caused by my defenses, to reaching out to people, loving them, giving myself.

The depressing list could be long. I note these few in order to make specific application of the hopeful promise,

> I will make up to you for the years that the locust has eaten.

All the spiritual/emotional rubbish I carry—the scars—*He will make up to me.*

It has seemed necessary, for a while, to take a long, hard look at the locusts of the past and to become conscious of what they have eaten in my life. I felt guilty about spending so much time getting to know these destroyers, until I saw how much Joel concentrates on them. He spends nearly two full chapters of his three-chapter prophecy describing the locusts and their devouring ways and why they have come. So my guilty feelings are unfounded. To understand what God is doing in my present, I must understand and appreciate what He has permitted in my past.

The locusts are the natural results of sin. They have left awesome desolation and hunger and poverty and despair in their path. All the wicked, warped, and painful patterns of my life today are the work of those swarming, stripping, creeping, and gnawing acridians.

How barren sin has left me!

As a child I toyed with it. It was given to me as a family legacy. My church failed to see how deep its effects had really gone and, from its own sin-damaged perceptions, distorted my perception of the Only Hope. None of us realized how stripped and ruined we were.

I see it more clearly now. The comprehension I now have of sin's ravages in my personality is like touching a mountain in the dark. I know I have seen only the tiniest bit of the hulking alp of the tragedy. The devastation is so great—in us all! How can we help but pity and empathize with one another in our miserable condition?

But . . .

The word from the Lord for today is that there is for us who are returning to Him, a new day so gloriously full of promise it's scarcely believable.

Listen man: Face squarely the tragic devastation left by the locusts. And while you are getting a good look, hear this:

> I will make up to you for the years
> That the swarming, creeping, stripping, gnawing locusts
>   (the varied and painful consequences of sin)
>   have eaten.
> I will make up
>   what has been destroyed in you by the choices of the past.

Apply that, man, to every destructive pattern still clinging to your life. . . . To those hair-trigger emotions that leap up within you without a chance to choose . . . To the habits of deceit by which you fool yourself and others . . . To the unbidden fears that devour your happy moments . . . To the inner responses that assure failure in relationships and ministry . . . To the negative and self-defeating feelings you feel for yourself.

The past ("the years") and everything that still hangs on you from it—

> *I will make up to you!*

The KJV reads, "I will *restore* the years."

How is it possible? To me they are irretrievably lost.

But to the One who inhabits eternity they are part of now. They are in His hands like today. He lived them with me, even when I was unaware of His presence.

I cannot go back to change anything, to correct the gross errors which set this wrong course to which my emotions so stubbornly adhere, or to plant pure seed to replace the rotten roots which began growing then. I can do nothing about those years except to offer them as part of the living sacrifice of myself to Him. And then wait for the promise.

——— • ———

Your love is great!
Your grace is fathomless!
The work of Your cross and the promise of Your emptied tomb reach to unimaginable lengths to save people.

Here . . . You take my years. Take everything I have kept from them. They are part of what I am. And now everything I am is Yours.

Return to Sovereignty

The good news is that our lost sovereignty can be restored to us. Sin—the act, the behavioral habitude, or "the antiquity of error"[14]—involves loss of personal sovereignty and freedom. Grace—as worked out in the life, death, and resurrection of Jesus and the Pentecostal invasion of the Holy Spirit—aims to reinstate the lost dominion.

Jesus promises: "If you hold to my teaching, you are really my disciples. Then you will know the truth, and the truth will set you free . . . I tell you the truth, everyone who sins is a slave to sin. Now a slave has no permanent place in the family, but a son belongs to it forever. So, if the Son sets you free, you will be free indeed" (John 8:31–36).

Paul writes: "Those who receive God's abundant provision of grace and of the gift of righteousness reign in life through the one man, Jesus Christ" (Rom. 5:17). "It is for freedom that Christ has set us free. Stand firm, then, and do not let yourselves be burdened again by a yoke of slavery" (Gal. 5:1).

James exhorts: "Let the process go on until . . . endurance is fully developed, and you will find you have become men of mature character with the right sort of independence" (James 1:4 Phillips).

The final fruit of the Spirit is a quality called "self control" (Gal. 5:23).

The New Testament abounds with references to the fact that we shall ultimately reign with Christ, judge angels, and administer important aspects of the kingdom-world (Luke 22:29–30; 2 Tim. 2:12; 1 Cor. 6:3; Rev. 1:6; 5:9–10; 20:4–6; 22:5). Our destiny, in Jesus, is total restoration of the human sovereignty of which the madness of sin has stripped us, in every area of life and every facet of human personality.

The Nebuchadnezzar-story ends happily with the re-establishment of the king, much wiser and less arrogant for his seven-year detour into the terrifying world of insanity. He describes what was involved in his healing and restoration (Dan. 4:2-4; 34-37). Progress toward sound emotional and spiritual health is marked by the following phenomena:

1. *The worship of God for who He is (Dan. 4:34-35, 37).*

Nebuchadnezzar has changed in the way he perceives God. Before, He was one of "the holy gods" (vv. 9, 18). Afterwards, He is "the Most High God ... who lives forever" and "the King of Heaven," whom the emperor blesses, praises, honors, and exalts.

True healing necessarily involves healing of one's perception of God, until the God one worships and relates to is, in fact, the true God, not the distorted image of God transmitted to us by pagan society, faulty parental modeling, or misguided religion.

Much of my life I have spent in running battle with a capricious, sometimes vicious, unpredictable, unreasonable conception of God. An image graven on my subconscious mind in unwitting violation of the Second Commandment, by manipulative and confused authority figures, who, in fact, were etching into my spirit their own image rather than His. Ascribing worth to such a god is most unnatural. Terror, hatred, and defensiveness are more appropriate.

Thank God! He has given us His personal image to look at—Jesus. Jesus is capable of correcting all our primal misconceptions. Healing becomes tangible as one's inner feeling-perception of diety becomes more and more like Jesus.

And as wholeness displaces sickness, worship is no longer mere liturgizing, intellectualizing and verbalizing, but is expressed as genuine love for God. When I am whole, I will say, "God, I love You," and my whole emotional, intellectual, psychological, spiritual, and physical being will agree (Luke 10:27).

2. *The acknowledgment of the sovereignty of God over the details of life (Dan. 4:2-3; 24-35).*

In his preface to the story, Nebuchadnezzar evaluates his seven-year bout with psychosis in a surprising way:

It has seemed good to me to declare the signs and wonders which the Most High God has done for me. How great are His signs, And how many are His wonders! (vv. 2–3, NASB).

Emotional healing is marked by freedom to praise God for His sovereign acts in our lives—even for emotional defects resulting from universal laws which His goodness has established.

Vain attempts to "slap God's hand" as He disciplines (v. 35) subside with return of health. One becomes able to rest in the stream of His sovereign working, flowing easily, resistlessly with the currents of His Father-will. At the apex of wholeness, the human mind is able to comprehend the beauty of God's disciplining (Heb. 12:5–11; 2 Cor. 4:7–11). Silent confidence replaces the "inevitable" questions which accompany illness, failure, or weakness: "What hast Thou done? (Dan. 4:35 NASB). Or, as it has often come from my mouth: "What are You trying to do to me, God?"

God is not required to meet our demands for a "satisfactory explanation." Once delivered of ill-health, even when I don't understand His action or seeming inaction, I will yet love Him and know that He is good.

Acknowledgment of sovereignty also implies submission in the practical matters of daily life. Rebellion equals anxiety, tension, fear—sickness of spirit. Submission equals peace with God, a sense of being cared for, a sense of direction, a sense of well-being—spiritual wholeness.

3. *The return of reason (Dan. 4:34, 36).*

Almost everyone in our culture suffers, to one degree or another, a specific spiritual malady which seriously hampers our ability to make sound judgments. Psychologists refer to it as "separation of intellect and emotions."

We have been taught to deny our feelings, and to rely solely on the organization of intellectual information in making choices. Feelings are untrustworthy, we have been led to believe. Only "cool logic" is reliable. Men especially, but not exclusively, have been taught to bury their tenderer sensibilities (i.e., "Big boys don't cry"). In order to produce achievers in a competitive society, many parents have withheld the tender expressions of affection and approval, and have reared generations composed largely of high intellectual achievers, who have never learned to feel, and angry emotional cripples, who simply could not develop in such a feeling-vacuum.

Every human being has feelings and our lives are ultimately controlled by them—whether we are "in touch" with them or not. We have little or no control over the effect of emotions that we do not allow ourselves to feel and express, but they affect our behavior and our relationships nonetheless.

By practiced denial of true feelings we have cut ourselves off from the valuable resources of intuition (i.e., "gut-level feelings") which often are reliable signals worth listening to, emerging from the subconscious mind. Sound reasoning involves a bringing together of intuition and intellectually organized information (logic) under the leadership of the Holy Spirit.

When one's spirit, mind, and emotions are well, he is fully able to feel his feelings, and to use them in the kind of sound reasoning which is vital to the exercise of sovereignty.

4. *The restoration of human glory (Dan. 4:36).*

In Nebuchadnezzar's case this involved a return to the throne, with the glory and majesty which were part of the office of King of Babylon. But his experience of restored human glory involved even more basic realities. For seven years he had run in the wild with "the mind of a beast" (v. 16 NASB). There seemed to be little left about him that was human. His healing was marked, literally, by a return to humanness.

The Bible promises, in Jesus, complete restoration of the splendor that is man:

> There is a place where someone has testified:
>
> > "What is man that you are concerned about him,
> >   or the son of man that you should care for him?
> > You made him [man] a little lower than the angels;[15]
> >   you crowned him with glory and honor
> >   and put everything under his feet."
>
> In putting everything under him [man], God left nothing that is not subject to him. Yet at present we do not see everything subject to him. But we see Jesus, who was

made a little lower than the angels, now crowned with glory and honor (Heb. 2:6-9, brackets added).

The splendor of being human is seen in Jesus, the man. Among the rest of us, even the most whole, none has yet reached the visible pinnacle of human glory upon which He lived. But the process of our transformation into His exact likeness is presently going on . . .

> We, who with unveiled faces all reflect the Lord's glory, are being transformed into his likeness with ever-increasing glory, which comes from the Lord, who is the Spirit (2 Cor. 3:18).

The nearer we approach to full health, the more we become like Jesus, the more authentically human we become. There is something wonderful about being human. To become whole is *not* to be changed into something else. To be whole is to be fully human with everything good that means.

Rediscovery of the splendor (i.e., worthiness and acceptedness) of our human destiny brings joy and hope into our lives. As spiritual normalcy returns, the old parental and diabolical tapes which helped to undermine this sense of splendor are gradually erased, forgiven, or proved false. A new self-respect emerges, based on truth and grace. A healthy self-love restores confidence. It feels good to be alive and to be me! And from this restored base of "okayness" with God and my humanness, I can begin to become self-forgetful in reaching out and responding to others . . .

> Love your neighbor as yourself (Rom. 13:9).

5. *The restoration of relationships damaged by spiritual sickness (Dan. 4:36).*

Courtiers who, in fear, had driven him from them, now begin again to seek Nebuchadnezzar.

The relational signal which announces emotional soundness is *love* (Luke 10:27-28). If one is growing up in love—including the capacity to make loving choices and to develop close, caring relationships with others—one is getting over being sick. Unhealed relationship problems, unforgiveness, and unwillingness or inability to be reconciled are symptoms of spiritual ill-health.

For many years, sensitive people said to me, "We cannot get close to you. You will not allow us to love you." It always hurt. And I always denied it. But as I have come to know the truth about myself I have discovered that they were reading me correctly. Experiences with rejection and pain in early-life relationships had indeed built into me a subconscious resistance (based on fear) to letting people know me and accepting their love. I would permit them to come just so far. Then they would run into a wall with a sign on it saying, "No closer!" Behind the wall was a frightened child promising himself, "I won't let myself be hurt again."

For a human being, especially a follower of Jesus, this is a serious problem. Love and healthy relatedness is what we are about as Christians (see John 13:34–35). As health comes, I will find new freedom to develop as a lover in Jesus' style.

6. *The re-establishment of personal sovereignty (Dan. 4:36).*

Nebuchadnezzar's return to the throne was only part of the restoration of his autonomy. What had been lost in his mind-snapping egomania was not merely control of the empire, but control of himself. Personal or human sovereignty must be restored before imperial sovereignty can return.

Self-control is the final fruit of the Spirit (Gal. 5:23). Freedom of choice, which places one in the position to select the course he will take in every situation is the key characteristic of personal emotional and spiritual health. Ironically, this unchained world of true freedom opens only to those who willingly bow in surrender to the sovereignty of God. Under His personal, practical rule in their lives, rightful human dominion is reinstated.

Only the free can choose to be "angry and sin not," as Ephesians 4:26 (KJV) instructs; or to trust in the very presence of personal fear, as David sings of it in Psalm 56:3; or to "clothe yourselves with compassion, kindness, humility, gentleness and patience" after having chosen to "rid yourselves of . . . anger, rage, malice, slander and filthy language," as Colossians 3:8, 12 exhorts.

As emotional soundness comes, compulsions disappear.

When I am serving someone or laying down my life for any person or cause, it will no longer be because I am being forced by some inner neurotic dependency, some unhealed need for approval.

Instead, in true liberty, I shall be able, like my Savior and Model, to freely choose to give—even to surrender my own freedom if necessary—in a servanthood which springs not from fear or guilt or a need to control others, but from love.

CHAPTER 13

Between the Red Sea and Mount Sinai

'Come near before the Lord, for He has heard your grumblings.'

And it came about as Aaron spoke to the whole congregation of the sons of Israel, that they looked toward the wilderness, and behold, the glory of the Lord appeared in the cloud.

And the Lord spoke to Moses, saying, 'I have heard the grumblings of the sons of Israel; speak to them, saying, "At twilight you shall eat meat, and in the morning you shall be filled with bread; and you shall know that I am the Lord your God"' (Exod. 16:9–12 NASB).

"The Ever-Whirling Wheels of Change"

Cardinal John Henry Newman said: "To live is to change, and to be perfect is to have changed often."

There is no growth without change. There is no progress, no maturing, no renewing, no re-forming without change. And yet change is seldom comfortable. Usually it is painful. The fearful resist it. As though they wished to remain children forever.

Alvin Toffler suggests that when too much change comes too rapidly and responses to too many strange, new stimuli are demanded in too short a time, disorientation sets in. An emotional disorder develops, which he calls "future shock."

> The last two months have been horrendous! I'm reeling from them, groping to ascertain their meaning and the

> meaning of the milieu of emptiness, lostness, and loneliness which blankets my life like a killer-smog.
>
> The way I have been feeling and responding to my situation, you would think I had left behind—at the house on Pasadena Avenue—all my security, worth, and hope. I have been roaring at the kids. Berating myself. Lashing out at Audrey. Feeling forsaken by God. My mind is in a state of dark confusion.
>
> The truth is, I love my kids. I think they are the best kids a man could have. I have been thankful for my wife, and inwardly, I understand why she cannot meet my unmeetable needs. But she thinks I do not love her, that I blame her, that she is not adequate. It is not surprising she's confused. I am woefully confused.
>
> The heart of the matter is, I'm filled with fear. Terrified. I feel desperately alone. I am at the end of my tether—in fact, my tether seems to have broken loose and I'm dragging it with me on my erratic course.

It seemed, at the time I wrote that, that the deliberate process of gradual change my family and I had been involved in for some twelve years had suddenly been shifted, by unseen hands, into high gear. Major changes were coming into our lives in breathless succession. The process was out of my hands. It was like being carried along by a flash flood. As security after security was swept away, I flailed and fought to find anything at all to cling to—but the flood was stronger and always won. I was helpless to keep emotionally abreast of its dizzying swirl.

A dozen years of "church renewal" had already significantly changed my "role in life." I had eased gradually out of "dominant pastor" status in the church. Believer-priests were discovering their roles as each other's ministers (1 Peter 2:4–5). Many things in the church had undergone healthy metamorphosis to give space for developing priests to serve one another. Small groups cared for many of the typical "hand holding" functions of the pastor. They had also begun to fulfill more and more of a counseling ministry which had previously been "all mine." They also carried on teaching and discipling functions, which formerly were part of my professional job description. Church meetings had gradually undergone change to make them a setting for ministry by the members of the Royal Priesthood. The "indispensibility" of my leadership in those meetings had become a thing of the past.[1]

Team pastoral leadership had replaced the conventional single-pastor structure. After a painstaking process of several years, a team of elders (pastors) drawn from the congregation itself, was now shepherding the church together. From the traditional viewpoint, I had effectively "worked myself out of a job," and was well into the process of trying to find my place as a member of the team.[2]

These changes in my official position had thrust me into a search for a personal identity less closely bound to the professional pastoral role. The church had become a caring, supportive family. They freed and encouraged me to face some interior conflicts that the restrictive script of the traditional role had previously kept me from addressing.

Sometimes it seems ironic that the church I led into renewal should now lead me into renewal. But thinking back, I remember that, from the beginning, one of my chief motives for seeking change in the church was my own unmet spiritual and emotional needs. There were deep hungers in me which I envisioned being satisfied by the kind of church life described in the Book of Acts. I needed the loving, caring, supporting reality visible in the New Testament Church. I yearned to know Christ the way they seemed to know Him and to experience the Holy Spirit the way they seemed to experience Him. So I set out to see if the church could be changed so it could know again its early power and life. The quest grew not alone from the need of the church, but from my own thirst for wholeness.

Hence, surrounded by a family of ministering priests, I dared to look deeply at myself. At a moment coinciding with God's sovereign design, the Holy Spirit, without asking my permission, ripped the lid off a secret inner cache of untreated spiritual garbage which was hindering my spiritual progress. The barriers to obedience He unmasked had been destructive beyond description, and, to further intensify the impact of the moment,

I had to admit that I did not know how to deal with them.

At that point I made some choices.

I decided to involve myself in a small, intense knot of believers committed to a program of "prayer therapy," to deal with the painful emotional issues of their lives. I determined to let them know me. In addition, I sought the help of a trusted Christian counselor. Ultimately I came to believe that to be emotionally healed is one of the "rights" offered us by the grace of God and I committed myself to pursue inner wholeness and spiritual liberty, at whatever cost or risks might be called for.

Thus was set in motion an intensive expedition into personal renewal, requiring soul-shaking changes in most of my personal relationships—including those with my wife, my God, and my church.

Change, I have found, is not as easy as saying it.

The revolution which now completely engulfs our lives has resulted from a volatile mixture of human choices and the sovereign circumstantial arrangements of God. About a year ago, the forces of change which had been set in motion in my life and the life of the church met the forces of resistance to change which are inherent in all human institutions. The result was a "big bang" which accelerated the "ever whirling wheels of change"[3] to breathless speed.

In the space of a few weeks, added to the fundamental restructuring I've described were these radical alterations:

Sensing the leadership of the Spirit (through consensus of the elders) to do so, our congregation returned the keys of its buildings to the denomination, moved out, and began meeting in several "house churches," instead of a single location. So, the buildings I had helped to build, the office to which I had gone nearly every day for more than a dozen years, the institution over which I had brooded and worried and watched and around which so much of my life had revolved, was instantly "off limits," no longer a part of my life or work. I had thought I was ready. Organizationally and philosophically I was. It was the right thing to do at the right time. But emotionally I had lost a precious heirloom to which I was sentimentally attached. And I mourned my loss.

Our appeal to be allowed to remain within the denominational structure was denied on the grounds that our unorthodox new form was too far from "the denominational norm." Audrey and I found ourselves outside the organization with which we had been associated all our lives. A lifetime of relationships was instantly shattered. It was heartbreaking to discover that some friendships we had thought were personal and genuine were, in fact, only part of the institutional facade. When institutional membership was severed, love died. I had thought I was ready. The non-conforming direction we had been taking had always held the potential of censure or expulsion, and I knew it. But when it came, the sense of rejection and loss was overwhelming. My "fostering mother" had thrown me out and branded my work "unapproved." I grieved as though someone dear to me had died.

(A short time later some denominational brothers in the neighboring California District, in a costly expression of love, worked for my reinstatement in the "mother church" by arranging for me to be received into their district. Though, in the process, I had been effectively "weaned" from dependence on the denomination, I felt I could only welcome this expression of personal caring. So six months after the break, I rejoined the denomination with full ministerial standing.)

Separation from the denomination meant that our house for fourteen years—a parsonage—would need to be vacated in sixty days. In a beautiful way, the Lord affirmed His intention to care for us, in the way He supplied us with a pleasant place to live at very reasonable cost. But so much of our lives had taken place in and around that parsonage! It was the only home two of my children had ever known. Charity Joy was born while we lived there. Now it became a symbol of rejection. I had boasted, "I'm not attached to anything earthly. God can have it all!" But I cried for three days while cleaning the place after we moved out. Every room was a clutter of memories I couldn't cleanse from my shattered spirit.

The new house was small. I couldn't find anything. Everything I needed was, apparently, "in storage." I kept longing to "go back home" (i.e., back to the house on Pasadena Avenue).

Our oldest daughter, Christine, with her husband, Vern,

had been living with us in the house on Pasadena for about four months, during a crisis of disappointment and financial struggle. Chris and I had had time together during those months—time together that had been stolen from us by my pastoral busyness when she was a little girl. It was good for us to eat breakfast together every day and to talk. I loved having her around. About a month before our move, she and Vern found an apartment and moved out. I missed them.

During the same period, our foster daughter, Reba, was going through a difficult time leading to a divorce. Her three-year-old daughter (our "foster grand-daughter," if you will) lived with us for several weeks prior to the divorce. Her mother was able to take her back, coincidentally, at the very same time all the other changes were happening. We all missed her. It was, for me, another necessary-but-painful change.

For Audrey, this time held special, positive changes. In December, just before we left our old neighborhood, she completed her Bachelor of Science degree at Grand Canyon College. In January she re-entered her career as a teacher, taking a position at Scottsdale Christian Academy teaching third grade. This fulfilment of her personal dreams was also fulfilment of her commitment to help me discover my true giftedness and my freedom.

This meant that during these weeks of intense upheaval, moving, and getting acclimated to our new living situation, she was busy, excited, thriving on new challenges. It was precisely what she needed. A special gift at a special time. But from my perspective, she was not there to talk to during the day any more. And I felt more alone than ever. I was jealous of her new job. She was finding herself in an exciting new career. I was lost, untethered, uprooted, and disoriented—trying to figure out what to do next. I spent my days alone in the strange house. Trying to work. But I was hurting too badly to accomplish anything of worth.

Changes, changes, changes. New stimuli bombarding my reeling senses. Adjustments were demanded in too many basic aspects of life at once. I felt forsaken by God, rejected by people, useless, and angry. I was demoralized by guilt and fear. And I fell, for several weeks, into a traumatized state of depression that was like mourning. I cried and complained and I yelled at God. I broke things. I hurt more deeply than I have hurt since my mother died when I was a boy. I wanted very badly to die.

(By "the miracle of 20/20 hindsight" I now see that God had timed all these upheavals to accomplish specific purposes in my life. He simply removed—all at once—many of my most precious restraints, securities, and protective shields, to intensify the focus on my need for inner healing.)

The bitter irony of the situation was that these changes had unceremoniously plunked me into the kind of life-opportunity I had often said I *wanted*. Freedom. "No strings attached." No obligation to fulfill anyone's expectations. No time clock to punch.

I was free from church responsibilities.
I was free from denominational demands.
I was free from an office schedule.
I was free from concerns for buildings and property.
I was free from concerns about appearances.
I was free from institutional concerns.
I was free to pursue my writing.
I was free to be with my family.
I was free to take time for personal growth.

Presumably, I could do whatever I wanted, whenever I wanted.

But . . . freedom is not merely a physical setting, it is a mindset.

Freedom Is Tough Too

This morning I woke with the same plaguing sense of despair. I begged God to help me understand what is happening to me—this combination of grief, dread of the future, loneliness, and bitterness.

An insight was given.

I began to sense a unique kind of identification with the children of Israel just after their escape from slavery in Egypt (Exod. 16–18). I think I understand their problem.

Their grumbling is infamous.

But . . . was it simply that they were terrible, ungrateful wretches, complaining for no reason and wanting to go back because they hated God? They may have been all those things and more. But there *was* a cause. No, not a cause good enough to justify their rebelliousness and their interminable bitching. Yes, they should have trusted God after all He had shown them of His love and power.

But, I want to plead their case for a moment. Remember: In Egypt their lives were bitter, but they were also secure. Slavery is hell. But freedom . . . freedom is tough too. Especially if one has spent his entire life in slavery.

In Egypt, when you got up in the morning, you always knew what you were going to do, what time they expected you at the mud-pits, what the consequences were of not showing up, and . . . where the next meal was coming from. Pharaoh's miserable ration of leek-and-onion soup was horrible and boring, but it was always there. The future was charted. You knew exactly where you were going and how to get there. It was really "nowhere," but there was a kind of security. Life was structured, predictable, uncomplicated. The decisions were all made by someone else. Pharaoh even fought your battles for you.

Now you are out here in this unfamiliar wilderness. You fight your own battles. You are responsible for your own decisions.

Some vague promises have been noised about concerning a "promised land," but all that is visible to the eye is a wispy cloud and a flickering fire. And no one is saying in advance which direction to go next.

The next meal is sometimes late in arriving and comes from strange new sources in strange new packaging. It's good food, but it takes some getting used to.

There is a strange emptiness—like loneliness—out here away from Egyptian civilization. You feel separated, cut loose from the predictable structures that previously gave order to life. You hated those structures and what they did to you . . . but *they were there*.

And right now, with the Red Sea behind and Sinai ahead, there are no structures to tell you what you are to do today.

And none to tell whether or not you are accomplishing anything. And none to tell you what your place is or where you fit into the scheme of things.

There are no deadlines to meet. No expectations to fulfill. No mud to make into bricks and nothing to build that is visible to the naked eye. Nothing concrete in which to take pride or about which to feel good. No reports to file on numbers of bricks made and laid, or hours worked, or tombs constructed.

There's just that flimsy cloud and that dancing, unsteady flame, and a single, muted voice stuttering, "F-f-follow m-me."

If I am free, if slavery is behind me . . . why do I feel like crying?

I get up in the morning and have to decide what I should do today. And what I should do with the rest of my life. The system once told me. And there was security in knowing—even though I did not always do what the system suggested. But now the system has regurgitated me out onto this dry land. I have escaped that old bondage, into "freedom." And I am lonely. Lost. Uncertain. Afraid that the trek across this wasteland leads nowhere.

I wake in the middle of the night and I cry in desperation and fear.

Audrey has a new structure filled with expectation and a new standard for measuring her achievements. It consumes her strength every day. It gives her purpose, security, and worth, and leaves her no time for grief.

I am free from structure. It's called "free lancing." It's what I am supposed to be doing for a living. I am free from anyone telling me what to do. Free to do my own thing. Free from reporting to anyone.

Free to . . . to . . . ?

Free to wander off across my spiritual desert, get lost, and die under a cactus called "How I feel about myself."

Lord, is there a new structure anywhere into which I need to be fitting? If it is possible to live without structure and be happy, please lead me to that happy dimension of full emancipation. By what, in that case, shall I measure success or failure? Or the quality of my relationship with You? At this moment, from my side, our relationship seems wispy and unsteady—a changeable white cloud, a dancing, flickering, uncertain flame.

Is there a Sinai ahead where You will outline the structure You have designed for me in which to be secure and to accomplish Your purpose too? Am I in that no man's land between the Red Sea and the Mountain of God? For Israel it was a three-month wait (Exod. 19:1). If that is Your timetable for me, by April I ought to know something, I ought to have a new sense of direction.

I'm not sure I can hold on 'til then.

Arrival at Sinai

Like the mythical Phoenix, a new structure began to emerge from the ashes of the old. Tentative at first. In April.

I joined the trek from the crimson sea of God's emancipation (Exod. 15:22) through Marah's bitterness—which God sweetened (vv. 23–25), Sin Desert's hunger—which God satisfied (ch. 16), Rephidim's thirst—which God quenched (17:1–6), and Amalek's see-saw attacks—which God enabled them to repel (vv. 8–16), to the Mountain of God (19:1–2). Upon arrival at Sinai, God spoke into being the basic principles of the new structure.

In Exodus 20, the Lord replaces the death-dealing structure of slavery with the life-giving structure of response to God. Characteristics of the new "Sinai structure" are:

1. *Freedom.* The new order is not intended to be at all like the former slavery.

> I am the Lord your God, who brought you . . . out of the house of slavery (Exod. 20:2 NASB).

In His prologue to the "Mosaic Covenant" God reveals His dream (Exod. 19:3–6). He has no wish to institutionalize a dutiful, rigid, hidebound, joyless, drudgery-of-a-religion that will weigh down like an impossible ox-yoke bending the necks and rubbing raw the shoulders of an unwilling people. As God, He knows in advance that most will never share with Him the personal intimacy He longs to share with them. Instead, they will become enslaved all over again—this time, legalistically entangled in mere performance of the shadowy pictures of divine reality He is about to show them (Heb. 10:1). Most will miss His Reality for their own lives amid enchaining institutions and traditions which people will build up around God's beautiful pictures.

But freedom from slavery was always God's dream for them. If, as one of God's people, I am enslaved or trapped, something is wrong. I have given myself to a structure other than His.

Sometimes He leads the slaves out of Egypt physically. Sometimes He recognizes the legitimacy of the physical relationships which are the milieu of our slavery (i.e., a difficult marriage, family responsibilities, financial obligations, even His own instructions) but seeks to change our perspective so that we may be His freedmen in spirit and relationship, without forsaking God-given responsibility. My most binding chains, I have discovered, are the guilts and fears that keep me from being who I am in my circumstances—not the circumstances themselves. God wants me to be free.

2. *Relationship.* The new structure is to be based on loving faithful interaction with God Himself.

> I, the Lord your God, am ... jealous ... showing *lovingkindness* ... to those who *love* Me ... (Exod. 20:5–6 NASB, italics added).

The core of biblical life-structure is always relationship with God. Its chief mark is a zealous[4] love flowing back and forth between the Lord and His beloved. In this relationship there is two-way communication on the level of reality. The relationship is, therefore, dynamic, growing, changing, as new insights break in, new experiences come, new intimacy develops.

The Sinai-structure is an inspirited order based on listening to the voice of God speaking, personally guiding the practical affairs of life, every day (Exod. 19:5; Deut. 13:4; 15:5; 30:20; Ps. 95:7–8). No precedent or protocol is to speak with more authority than His voice. No concretized pattern, no prescripted set of role expectations is to have exclusive direction over one's actions in any area of life or work.

My new life-structure is not in the rigid systems which religious people have built up around their static perceptions of biblical truth. I am not, as one of His people, to shape my life according to the familiar, comfortable, acceptable, secure preconceptions and formulas of religion. But I look for life's order and meaning in a daily life of response to the voice of God heard in the context of lively friendship with Him.

3. *Response.* The new structure develops as a response to the knowledge of who God is, what He has done, and what He is doing for His people.

> You yourselves have seen what I did to the Egyptians, and how I bore you on eagles' wings, and brought you to Myself (Exod. 19:4 NASB). I am the Lord your God, who brought you out of the land of Egypt, out of the house of slavery (Exod. 20:2 NASB).
> Now then (Exod. 19:5 NASB).

Here the Bible comes into focus for us. It is the authoritative revelation of what God has done for us, how He has loved and cared and provided for us. In the New Testament, in the face of Jesus Christ, we see clearly who God is, what His priorities and concerns and methods are, how He feels about us, and to what lengths He will go to save and free us.

The structure or formation of the believer's life is expected to take shape as a response to the grace of God:

> Therefore, I urge you, brothers, *in view of God's mercy,* to offer your bodies as living sacrifices, holy and pleasing to God—which is your spiritual worship [recognition of the worthiness of God] (Rom. 12:1, italics and brackets added).

(Paul had just spent eleven chapters describing God's mercy. Only then does he suggest the shape our lives are to take.)

John puts the response-lifestyle another way:

> We love *because He first loved us* (1 John 4:19, italics added).

The structure of my life is not one of frightened, reluctant, or mechanical obedience to arbitrary commandments. That is slavery. My life will have order and security if I seek to live daily in response to God. To me this means, among other things, continual exposure to the revelation of God's character and thinking found in His Word, the Bible. In this, I do not guiltily approach Scripture afraid to discover my discrepancies, nor do I determine doggedly that I will unemotionally obey each word without question. I search the Word to discover *Him*. As I come to know *Him* I can respond.

4. *Obedience based on trust*. The kind of response on which the biblical life-structure operates is obedience (i.e., living in keeping with the revealed wisdom of God because we believe that He knows us thoroughly and never forgets our best interests).

> Now then, if you will indeed obey my voice and keep my covenant (Exod. 19:5 NASB).

True wisdom is the practical acknowledgment that God, who made man and the universe in which he lives, alone understands the formula for freedom and abundant life. While God loves us and forgives our failures to live in harmony with His wisdom, abundant life and true liberation come into our daily human experience only to the extent that we actually do live by His precepts (see Exod. 19:5 NASB, "indeed"; also John 8:31-32; James 1:22; 2:14-26). His precepts, principles, and commandments are, in effect, keys to full, rich living.

In both Old and New Covenants are revelations of pure grace. Both the Ten Commandments (Exod. 20) and the Beatitudes (Matt. 5), for instance, are disclosures of the way to live full and free as human beings. Neither was ever intended to become a heavy burden, robbing people of the good things of life. Both are gracious gifts—divine secrets whispered into the ears of believers by the God who knows the mysteries of life, to give us a chance to live life at its best, in the midst of a rebel society which has lost the secret of life and cannot find it.

I did not as fully realize, until recently, that inner disharmony with divinely established universal principles is the cause of all the misery, despondency, guilt, fear, frustration, and hostility—the description of which has consumed so many pages of this book. Vital areas of my thinking, feeling, and living have been at dissonance with the thinking of God.

The pain and confusion with which I have struggled result from that dissonance.

After two years of "prayer therapy," many sessions of personal counseling, and many hours of Primal Integration Therapy, I have come to know myself comparatively well. I have begun to understand what happened to make me think and feel as I do. My awareness has grown that, when dealing with destructive feelings, unresolved emotional conflicts, buried personal intensities of various kinds, one is dealing with sin and its damage. The more I know myself—the more I affirm in the inner man my dire need of God's grace and Jesus' blood, and the more convinced I become that *the internalization of God's revealed truth and the application of all of God's principles to the totality of my interior and exterior life, constitutes the only workable course to wholeness and richness of life.*

Obedience and love and response to God in the inner and outer man of my life will be required if ever I expect to have proper self-esteem, enjoy a sound sense of fulfilment and hope, or approach daily living with a healthy measure of confidence and peace.

> For me, two large barriers have barred the way to a life lived in response to the voice of God:
> 1. I have for so long lived out fear-powered, faithless patterns of response, that, even when I know what God wants, I, at first, seem incapable of breaking my old emotional habits, in order to respond to His speaking Word.
>
> Here is an example: Since childhood I have been confused about love. My automatic hang-up works like this: When someone says, "I love you," I instinctively mistrust him. I subconsciously expect him to follow that statement by inflicting pain upon me. My conditioned responses tell me: To love is to punish. My childhood God said, "I love you." And then threatened to send me to hell for even one failure to live according to His known instructions! My parents said, "I love you." And then proceeded to punish me ("Because we love you"). To me, it was very confusing. As a result, I do not even trust *myself* to say "I love you," and mean it.
>
> Intellectually, I understand that God tells us to love one

another (John 13:34-35). That is God's wisdom and one of the secrets to abundant living. But I have this secret malfunction which, though I certainly have not understood what was happening, has "automatically" thrown up defenses whenever anyone has tried to express affection for me—and which has, just as "automatically," made me feel hypocritical and dishonest when I have tried to express love.

While my "problem" doesn't nullify the divine principle nor relieve me of responsibility to give and receive love—it does make it very difficult to respond. Love, for me, has remained a painful experience and I have remained a cripple in the most important area of the Christian life! My only hope to experience the richness which full response to this Word from God would bring into my life, is for healing and change to come to the unseen, unconscious, automatic response-mechanism which persists in disrupting the harmony and joy of my relationships.

2. All my life I have lived, to one degree or another, in response to the walls of the established religious order and the expectations of people. These external walls are visible, feelable, and often very clearly defined. They often seem to "answer all the questions" about propriety, morality, piety, and so on. I know my way around in this old order, bounded by these familiar walls.

The new structure, with its practice of looking inside to my relationship with God, and of listening for God's voice for day-to-day direction, is so unfamiliar that I have no small difficulty hearing. It is easy (I can do it with my eyes shut and without thinking or trying) to fall back into my old habit of shaping my daily life to the acceptable structures of the status quo. And it is so natural to feel "at loose ends" in the new structure, with seemingly nothing to hang on to, nothing to guide me.

As we trembled at the foot of the Mountain of God, the Children of Israel and I struggled with a divinely disclosed life-structure quite foreign to our previous way of life. An aura of mingled excitement and fear set the tone for our response.

Jacob's offspring were bold to respond: "All that the Lord has spoken we will do!" (Exod. 19:8 NASB).

My response is a little more tentative, based on a growing comprehension that to walk with God in the freedom, relationship, and responsiveness He desires, will require penetrating repentence (change) and radical renewal (restructuring) well beyond my present state of spiritual maturity.

Embarkation

Father, if I am to bring off this new lifestyle of response to You, I will need help. I will need to be changed, deeply. I cannot seem to change myself. Show me, daily, how to do it.

> Whenever the cloud was lifted from over the tabernacle, afterward the sons of Israel would then set out; and in the place where the cloud settled down, there the sons of Israel would camp. At the voice of the Lord the sons of Israel would set out, and at the voice of the Lord they would camp; as long as the cloud settled over the tabernacle, they remained camped . . .
>
> Thus they set out from the mount of the Lord three day's journey, with ark of the covenant of the Lord journeying in front of them for the three days, to seek out a resting place for them. And the cloud of the Lord was over them by day, when they set out from the camp.
>
> Then it came about when the ark set out that Moses said,
> > "Rise up, O Lord!
> > And let Thine enemies be scattered,
> > And let those who hate Thee flee from Thy presence."
>
> And when it came to rest, he said,
> > "Return Thou, O Lord
> > To the myriad thousands of Israel."
>
> (Numbers 9:17–18; 10:33–36 NASB, slightly paraphrased to add marginal readings.)

Notes

CHAPTER 2
[1] Acts 2:42 NEB.

CHAPTER 4
[1] There can be little doubt that my perceptions of life under law is full of neurotic intensity, based on my own accumulative negative childhood experience with evangelical legalism. To that extent what I am sharing here may not be a biblically accurate representation of the teaching of Romans 7:1–6. What I am sharing is a *personal* response to insight which came to me for *personal* application in my life. I share it because I believe it is needed by others who may identify their own experiences with mine, and because I believe it is not inconsistent with the thrust of biblical revelation.

CHAPTER 5
[1] In *Handbook for Mission Groups* (Waco: Word Books, 1975), Gordon Cosby, founder of the Church of the Savior, Washington, D.C., talks about what the Bible teaches concerning personal uniqueness (1 Cor. 12). This section combines paraphrased excerpts from his book (Chapter 2, "Calling Forth the Gifts," pp. 70–85) with my own personal comments on the subject.

[2] Ibid., p. 73.

[3]Ibid., p. 73.
[4]Ibid., p. 75.
[5]Ibid., p. 74.
[6]Peale and Blanton, *Faith Is the Answer* (Pawling, N.Y.: Foundation for Christian Living, 1955).
[7]Oswald Chambers, *Still Higher for His Highest* (Grand Rapids: Zondervan, 1970), p. 156.
[8]Cecil Osborne, *The Art of Learning to Love Yourself* (Grand Rapids: Zondervan, 1976), p. 8.
[9]Cosby, *Handbook for Mission Groups*, p. 77.

CHAPTER 7

[1]Wheaton, Illinois: Tyndale House Publishers, 1978.
[2]A reference to one of my earlier books.

CHAPTER 9

[1]Cecil Osborne, *The Art of Learning to Love Yourself* (Grand Rapids: Zondervan, 1976), pp. 145-146.
[2]Cecil Osborne, *Release From Fear and Anxiety* (Grand Rapids: Zondervan, 1976).
[3]Osborne, *Love Yourself*, p. 144.
[4]Ibid., pp. 144-145.
[5]Primal Integration Therapy.
[6]"Connections" are insights into the reasons for certain feelings and into the ways in which primal feelings and primal patterns of response have carried over from early life to the present, thus clearing up confusion and providing "handles" for dealing with needed change.
[7]A padded bat used as an aid in expression of strong emotions during therapy.
[8]Even using the phrase, "In Jesus' name," or the words, "The blood of Jesus," as though there were "magic" in the words, makes me uneasy. Reminding ourselves of God's promises in order to strengthen faith has value, but I do not believe God is impressed with "passwords"—even if they are His own statements. The words are symbols for realities which

exist and are available to God's people without any requirement that mystical words be spoken. The benefits of the Gospel flow freely from His grace, powerfully won at the cross and the emptied tomb by His Son. Our part, as His children, is to believe His promises and seek single-hearted alignment with His revealed principles. When faith and alignment merge, we have received what He promised (John 15:4–7).

[9]Many who are thus engaged are not believers in Jesus Christ, nor part of His body. Some are. The fact that unconverted or unbelieving people could be involved in driving out evil spirits is substantiated by the New Testament itself. See Luke 11:19 and Acts 19:13, for example.

[10]Matthew 5:8.

[11]A rough quotation of Luke 10:27.

CHAPTER 10

[1]*The Analytical Greek Lexicon* (Grand Rapids: Zondervan, 1970).

[2]Ibid.

[3]Ibid.

[4]O'Shaughnessy, Toni-Lynn Maffucci (a student at Houghton College, Houghton, N.Y.), "Out of the Struggle," *Decision*, Nov. 1979.

[5]Ibid.

[6]Cowper, William, "There Is A Fountain Filled With Blood," *Hymns of the Living Faith* (Marion, Indiana: Wesleyan Publishing Association).

CHAPTER 11

[1]Copyright Yokefellows, Inc., Burlingame, California. Slip Y25b.

[2]Copyright Yokefellows, Inc., Burlingame, California. Slip Y136.

[3]Clyde Reid, *Celebrate the Temporary* (New York: Harper & Row, 1972), p. 42.

CHAPTER 12

[1] Daniel 4:10–17, adapted from NASB.
[2] Ibid., vv. 24–26.
[3] Ibid., v. 27.
[4] Ibid., v. 30.
[5] Ibid., vv. 31–32 (italics added).
[6] Ibid., v. 33.
[7] Ibid., vv. 34–37 (italics added).
[8] Osborne, *Learning to Love Yourself*, p. 101.
[9] The Hebrew word for mercy is *chesed*. According to Barclay, it means to get inside another person to know and experience what he is experiencing. *The Gospel of Matthew* (Philadelphia: The Westminster Press, 1975), Vol. 1, p. 103.
[10] "Prevenient grace" is a term popularized by John Wesley to designate all that God has done and is doing, completely apart from faith, to make it possible for sinners to find their way to Him.
[11] Cecil Osborne defines a neurosis as "a strong to severe overreaction" (*The Art of Learning to Love Yourself*, p. 66). It may be anger, fear, guilt, inferiority, aggression, or any number of normal human feelings which have become excessive, and thus distort reality.
[12] A term based on Heb. 12:1 KJV, "the sin which doth so easily beset us," used to refer to areas in a person's life in which he most easily and repeatedly falls into sin.
[13] Oswald Chambers, *Still Higher* (Grand Rapids: Zondervan, 1970), June 24.
[14] Cyprian, *circa* 250 A.D.
[15] In Psalm 8:5, from which this quotation is taken, the original Hebrew word is *Elohim*, one of the Old Testament names for God. There it reads: "You made him a little lower than God" (NASB).

CHAPTER 13

[1] For details on these changes see my book *Brethren, Hang Together* (Grand Rapids: Zondervan, 1979), pp. 259–264.
[2] Ibid., pp. 202–245.

[3] Spencer.
[4] In Hebrew, the word for "jealous" and "zealous" are the same word. In God's kind of loving, His jealousy comes out of His burning zeal for us.